GETTING IT ALL TOGETHER

Curriculum Integration in the Transition Years

The Metropolitan Toronto School Board

Pembroke Publishers Limited

Project Managers and Writers
Keith Hubbard, Dick Roberts

Writers
Bob Aitken, Debbie Fishman, Manon Gardner, Sue Ladoucer, Janet Phillips

Acknowledgements
This book is the outcome of our collaboration with dedicated educators who have shared their expertise and thoughtful reflections on classroom practice. We thank particularly Linda Hart-Hewins, Nanci Goldman, and Fran Parkin for their assistance in revising and adapting this special edition of *Getting It All Together.*

We are also indebted to the educators from the East York, Etobicoke, North York, Scarborough, Toronto, and City of York Boards of Education who participated in our advisory board and review panel.

Editor: Jessica M. Pegis

Design: Gail Ferreira Ng-A-Kien

Cover: John Zehethofer

Cover Photography: Ajay Photographics

Interior Photography: Robert Boehm, Alan Miller

©1995 The Metropolitan Toronto School Board

Pembroke Publishers
538 Hood Road
Markham, Ontario L3R 3K9

Canadian Cataloguing in Publication Data

Main entry under title:
Getting it all together : curriculum integration in the transition years

Includes biographical references.
ISBN 1-55138-059-5

1. Interdisciplinary approach in education.
2. Education, Secondary — Curricula.
   I. Hubbard, Keith, 1940– . II. Roberts, Dick. II. Metropolitan Toronto School Board.

LB1628.G47   1995   373.19   C95-931609-4

A catalogue record for this book is available from the British Library. Published in the UK by Drake Educational Associates, St. Fagan's Road, Fairwater, Cardiff CF5 3AE

Printed and bound in Canada

9 8 7 6 5 4 3 2 1

TABLE OF CONTENTS

INTRODUCTION

Teaching and Learning in the Transition Years

The purpose of this resource guide is to assist teachers in designing, developing, and delivering an integrated curriculum which meets the needs and interests of learners.

What Is Integration?

Integration may be defined as "the bringing or fitting together of parts into a whole." Curriculum integration involves bringing together the knowledge, skills, and perspectives of many subject areas to aid the exploration of a topic, theme, or issue that is relevant to the learner. Currently, a wide variety of integration models are used in our schools. These range from one teacher working in one classroom to school-wide initiatives. Whatever its form, integration must be planned, that is, based intentionally on teachers' understanding of the nature of knowledge and learning, the needs of the early adolescent learner, and the changing world.

To meet the needs of students in the transition years (grades 7–10), an integrated program is based on essential cross-curricular learnings which establish broad learning strands across the traditional subjects and the subject clusters (see page 8 for a diagram of clustering). Thus the program establishes a more "holistic" approach to student learning. Many teachers will find that this approach supports what they are already doing in the classroom, while at the same time providing a guide for further observation, thought, and action.

Why Integrate?

Historically, subject disciplines have been taught in isolation and have been based on specialization. However, because the body of knowledge associated with any one field is increasing at such a rapid rate, today's students must learn how to acquire and utilize information more efficiently. This is accomplished by learning how to make connections between similar concepts and skills shared by several disciplines. In fact, most of the challenges students will face in life will require this integrated response. In dealing with real-life situations, we need to look at the questions or issues as a whole, and to examine them in relation to ideas and information from a number of different areas. Moreover, a significant body of research supports the view that the mind naturally seeks patterns and connections in order to make sense of the world.

Integration has provided the vehicle for many teachers to make learning more meaningful for their students. It has allowed them opportunities to go beyond the textbook to make learning more significant and more rewarding for the young adolescent.

Well-planned integration has been shown to have important benefits for all participants. Studies indicate that integration increases mutual teacher support, and leads to more effective learning, improved student attitudes, faster identification and resolution of student problems, and improved teacher-student relationships (MacIver, 1990). An integrated curriculum is also one which is less likely to suffer from "overload" or fragmentation.

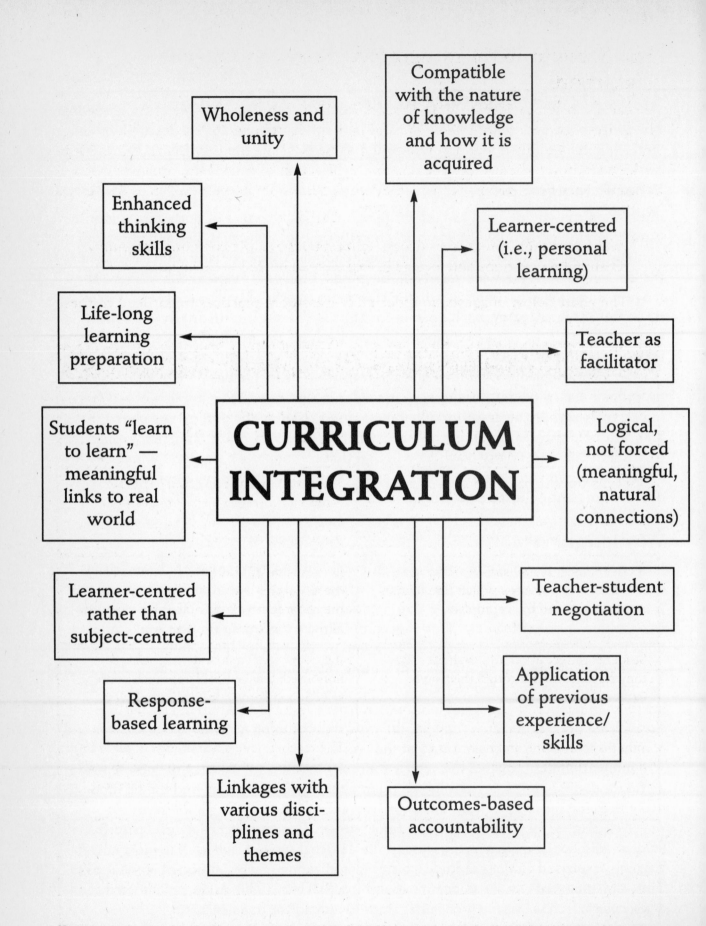

Wholeness and unity

Compatible with the nature of knowledge and how it is acquired

Enhanced thinking skills

Learner-centred (i.e., personal learning)

Life-long learning preparation

Teacher as facilitator

Students "learn to learn" — meaningful links to real world

CURRICULUM INTEGRATION

Logical, not forced (meaningful, natural connections)

Learner-centred rather than subject-centred

Teacher-student negotiation

Response-based learning

Application of previous experience/ skills

Linkages with various disciplines and themes

Outcomes-based accountability

The Student in an Integrated, Learner-Centred Classroom

As teachers begin to develop an integrated classroom program, the role of the student in the process requires serious thought. Within an integrated model, students' knowledge and interests are taken into account during all phases, i.e., program planning, decision-making regarding the use of time and space, selection of curriculum topics and activities, and evaluation. As one expert in the area of curriculum integration, James Beane, has written:

> Real curriculum integration occurs when young people confront personally meaningful questions and engage in experiences related to those questions.

The chart below suggests how desirable classroom practices might lead to these kinds of questions and experiences:

CLASSROOM ACTIVITIES ⟶	HOW INTEGRATION OCCURS
Students interact with their teacher(s), fellow students, and others, along with a variety of texts and media, as they construct meaning and develop understanding.	Students help choose the variety of texts and media which naturally extend beyond traditional subject boundaries.
Students work in pairs, groups, and as a class, on tasks which are increasingly of their own design. They share, extend, and evaluate one another's work.	Students' responsibility to design and extend each other's work implies their authority to do so, and does not restrict them to any one subject area.
Students read, write, speak, view, draw, and listen for purposes which they understand and intend to accomplish.	Because student **intention** is essential to these learning processes, the world beyond the classroom will inevitably be reflected in these functions and purposes.
Students reflect upon and evaluate what they have learned through their own explorations.	If student reflection and evaluation are honoured, teachers will approach content selection in some non-traditional ways.
What is to be done and how it is to be done are subject to negotiation.	The teacher develops methods of allowing learners to co-plan the curriculum, including resource areas, directions of learning, and assessment and evaluation.
Students use knowledge and reflect upon it in all areas of the curriculum, inside and outside the classroom. People from the community often visit the classroom and vice versa.	The teacher imagines how the class can make connections with other subject disciplines, aspects of the community, and aspects of other cultures.

The Integrated Program for Young Adolescents

4 SUBJECT AREAS	10 CROSS-CURRICULAR LEARNINGS

1 ARTS
- Dance
- Dramatic Arts
- Music
- Visual Arts

2 LANGUAGE
- English
- French
- Other Languages
- English as a Second Language

3 MATHEMATICS, SCIENCE, AND TECHNOLOGY
- Mathematics
- Science
- Technology

4 SELF AND SOCIETY
- Business Studies
- Family Studies
- Geography
- Guidance
- History
- Physical and Health Education

1 Language and Thinking Development

2 Mathematical Skills and Perspective

3 Scientific Knowledge and Perspective

4 Technological Knowledge and Perspective

5 Historical and Geographical Understanding and Cultural Identity

6 Global and Environmental Understanding

7 Social Responsibility and Human Rights

8 Relationship Between Learning and Working

9 Aesthetic Understanding and Artistic Expression

10 Personal Health and Well-Being

The Transition Years: The Broader Context

An integrated program for students in the transition years (grades 7 – 10) represents more than a mixed-ability/common curriculum. It also represents one aspect of a systematic restructuring of education. Many features of this program build on changes identified for younger children.

The need to embark upon a widespread restructuring of education arises from a number of observations and predictions about our changing society. These include:

- Family structure has changed. Many children born in the early '70s will see their parents separate before they are 20.
- Although the current labour market suffers from a high unemployment level, there is a shortage of skilled workers — an interesting paradox.
- Successful economies are now those in which people create value by applying knowledge to goods and services or by inventing better ways of performing old tasks.
- Immigration policies mean that developed countries will continue to receive a significant number of immigrants and refugees each year.
- Eighty percent of the jobs forecasted for the year 2000 do not currently exist.

Neither these changes nor the educational responses are unique to any particular region. Similar occurrences are taking place globally.

Basic Beliefs

Educational authorities have identified four basic beliefs to guide the process of change in education.

Accountability	A clear definition of what is expected of learners and what they actually achieve, along with clearer and more comprehensive reporting to the public.
Excellence	A commitment to high standards of achievement in our schools.
Equity	A commitment to removing established barriers and biases in school policies, programs, and practices.
Partnership	A firmer rooting of our schools in the communities they serve.

Lasting Change Equals Knowledge, Combined Effort, and Time

Acknowledged experts on effecting real change, such as Michael Fullan of the University of Toronto's Faculty of Education, agree that many elements must be brought together in order to reform complex systems. Within individual schools, establishing a collaborative school climate and fostering many innovations simultaneously are among the biggest issues. Those working towards reform will appreciate that bringing about lasting change takes time — usually two to three years. A number of key features in this process have been identified and are worth noting:

- Meaningful change occurs only when the people involved accept and facilitate that change. While structural change can be mandated, beliefs and behaviour cannot.
- All successes look like failures early in the process. Problems are inevitable and the skill needed to address them will be developed over time only through trial and error.
- "Ready, Fire, Aim" may be the most appropriate approach to strategic planning. Because the solutions to problems only emerge from the attempts to resolve them, strategic plans and visions will be continually revised and refined.
- Collaboration for its own sake is not the answer. The individual and the group are equally important in working toward change and in providing a needed variety of perspectives. It is particularly important to look for ways in which individuals can connect with innovation.
- The school, while it is the centre of change, needs the commitment and the resources of the system to succeed.
- The pace of change cannot be forced. Efforts to do so inevitably result in the neglect of vital personal or other elements.
- Within the first three years, there will be a number of spurts of advance and retreat. Attention to a problem-solving approach provides clues about when to hold back and when to press forward during this period.

MORAL: Innovations that are easily acquired are also easily dismissed.

— Adapted from Fullan and Miles, Getting Educational Reform Right; What Works, and What Doesn't, Phi Delta Kappan, June 1991.

The Transition Years: The Players

The most important aspect of an integrated program is not just the curriculum, but also the collaboration of many people to meet the needs of the adolescent learner. It is a challenging process, bringing together teachers, parents, and students to make learning meaningful.

Let's meet a few of the significant participants and look at some of their concerns and questions.

Teacher A

Teacher A is an experienced and successful teacher. Students enjoy going to this class and parents are pleased with their children's achievements.

This teacher is responsible for the delivery of four core subjects in a half-day program. In order to meet educational requirements, the teacher has carefully structured large blocks of time into subject-specific periods.

Having a reputation for innovation and the ability to accept challenge, Teacher A has been encouraged to look at ways of bringing curriculum integration into the classroom.

Over the next few weeks as he/she contemplates this idea, the following concerns surface:

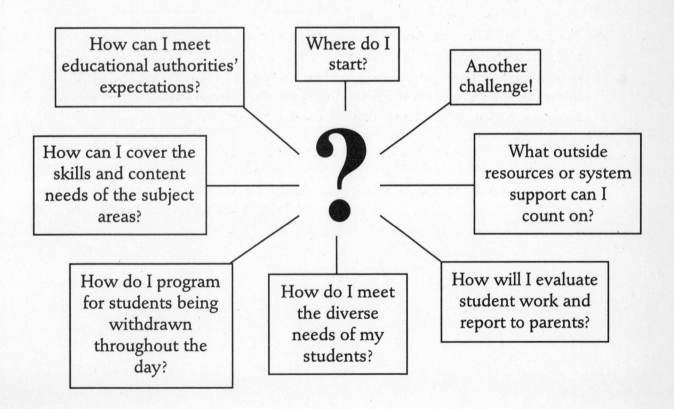

How can I meet educational authorities' expectations?

Where do I start?

Another challenge!

How can I cover the skills and content needs of the subject areas?

What outside resources or system support can I count on?

How do I program for students being withdrawn throughout the day?

How do I meet the diverse needs of my students?

How will I evaluate student work and report to parents?

Teacher B

Teacher B has special training in one subject area and is considered an expert in that field. This teacher has been teaching for many years and is highly respected by staff members, students, and parents. Teaching one subject in a rotary system allows the teacher to share expertise with a large number of students.

As a dedicated professional, Teacher B makes a consistent effort to remain current with educational change. Various articles and discussions dealing with curriculum integration have sparked a desire to know more. After some research several concerns have emerged:

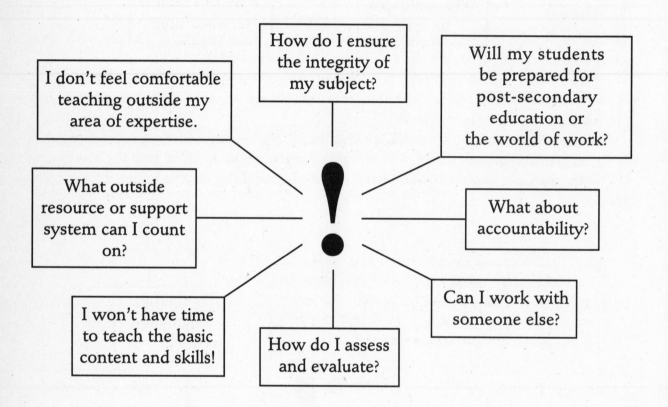

The Parent

Generally satisfied with and supportive of the public school system, this parent has been actively involved in the education of his/her children. One child is close to graduation and is doing very well. Two younger siblings will be affected by the educational changes in the transition years. Media reporting of educational restructuring as well as discussions with other parents and educators have generated the following concerns:

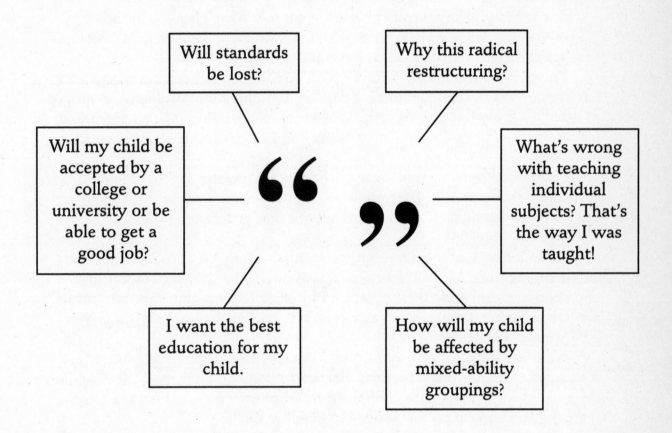

Will standards be lost?

Why this radical restructuring?

Will my child be accepted by a college or university or be able to get a good job?

What's wrong with teaching individual subjects? That's the way I was taught!

I want the best education for my child.

How will my child be affected by mixed-ability groupings?

Student X: "A Day in My Life"

This participant has a unique perspective since he/she will be involved in both planning and accomplishing the learning that is to take place during the young adolescent years. Student X thinks the following:

Woke up this morning a little late. Deciding what to wear is usually the biggest challenge of my day, and today is no exception. Looking just right, but not like you tried too hard, is real important. I'm way behind schedule now, but hey, I look great! No time for breakfast this morning — I'll just eat a big lunch.

Got to hurry, all my friends are waiting for me. We're all going to try out for the co-ed volleyball team before school. I think it's great that teachers offer lots of extra-curricular activities. Most kids take part in something.

The try-outs were great! I stayed to talk to the teacher after everyone had left and arrived in class just in time for the morning announcements. Boring, as usual! Halfway through the announcements someone leaned over and asked for the answers to the Period 2 homework and I suddenly realized I'd forgotten to do it!

First period is my favourite class. The teacher gives us lots of group work. Instead of giving us all the information, we are encouraged to investigate on our own. Maybe I'll have time to do some of that homework I didn't do!

Wrong!

Today's class was too interesting to spend doing homework. We dealt with global issues, amazing stuff like global warming. The whole class got into it and everyone expressed their opinion. This stuff has a major impact on how we live each day. I mean, you can't even step out of the house without your S.P.F. factor.

Well, it's trauma time. I sure hope I'm not embarrassed in front of my friends when homework is checked. I'm fairly smart and don't really need to do the extra work at home, but it counts for part of my grade so I always have it done. I guess I talked on the phone too long last night.

Hey, it turns out the homework won't be checked after all! Nobody understood the lesson yesterday. Review — yuk — I hate it. Same kids are up to the board again. I can't figure out why teachers always manage to pick the kids who truly don't understand the work. It's like they have to make a point or something. You could get really depressed about the whole thing and just quit trying. If we get time to work on our homework today, I'll do mine quick and then offer to help some of the other kids.

Lunch — my favourite time!

The kids I hang out with all have the same lunch time. We sit in the same place every day, eat mostly junk food and talk about everything — sports, music, clothes, dating. After lunch we usually sneak off to have a quick smoke. My parents would kill me if they found out I smoked, but most of my friends do it, so why not?

After lunch it's so hard to concentrate going from one class to another all afternoon. My mind wanders often in school, especially when the subject doesn't really turn me on. Who decides what we're supposed to learn in school anyway? It sure would be great if kids had more say in what we learn and how we learn it.

Whew, another day closer to the weekend. Gotta find my friends and do some serious planning! "Hey! Wanna come to my place till my parents get home from work?"

The concerns of Student X are summarized in the following diagram:

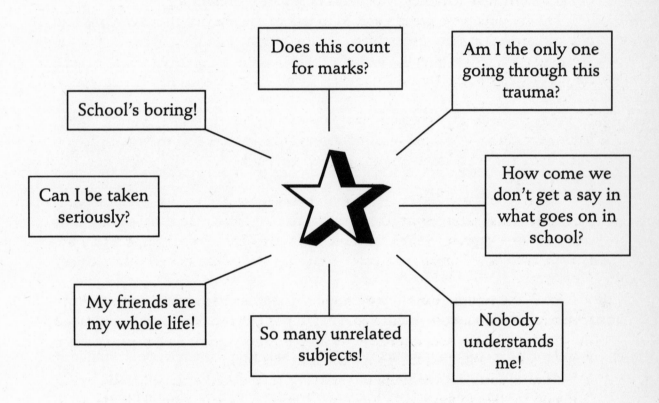

Curriculum Integration

When to Integrate?

Integration of the curriculum is an appropriate strategy in a variety of circumstances, but especially when:

- the focus is not on recalling information, but on analytic thinking and problem-solving, and issues that involve a variety of subjects
- students integrate knowledge and analyze relationships among subjects
- the emphasis is on the depth or quality of student understanding rather than the coverage of a quantity of information
- students' personal experiences and needs are seen as relevant to the curriculum
- the curriculum examines issues and concerns from the perspective of the world beyond the classroom using strategies appropriate to the task
- the curriculum provides opportunities for outcomes-based education including authentic assessment

> Real curriculum integration occurs when young people confront personally meaningful questions and engage in experiences related to those questions.
>
> — James Beane

When Not to Integrate?

Curriculum integration, while often desirable, is not an end in itself. Integration should be approached with caution when:

- the theme identified involves content or skills that are trivial or lacking in real significance for early adolescent learners
- the integration of several subjects seems artificial rather than natural
- the time involved in planning and delivering the model outweighs the goals achieved

Integration Models: The Rationale

This book focuses on three models for curriculum integration. The models are based on the developmental stages related to educational change. In other words, while some teachers are just beginning to think about integration, some are already experimenting with it, and some are totally immersed in it. The needs of teachers at each of these stages are very different.

The following diagrams for each integration model (pages 17 – 19) represent the various needs and the developmental stages outlined above. Movement from one model to the next allows teachers a clearer understanding of what is involved in delivering a truly integrated curriculum. The names of the models correspond to, and describe as closely as possible, the diagrammatic representations.

Within each model a variety of organizational approaches may be used. The sample outlines of the models which follow (pages 25 – 90) demonstrate only a few of the combinations possible (i.e., subject combinations, suggested activities, time lines). Note that the samples provide only skeletal outlines for organizing integration. In this way, teachers will be able to make substitutions easily depending upon expertise, teaching assignment, school structure, and available resources.

The chart on page 20 represents three ways of delivering the integration model based on the number of teachers and classroom type. On pages 21 – 22, a chart is provided that leads teacher and administrator through the various phases involved in making the transition to the integration models.

Model 1: Subject-Based

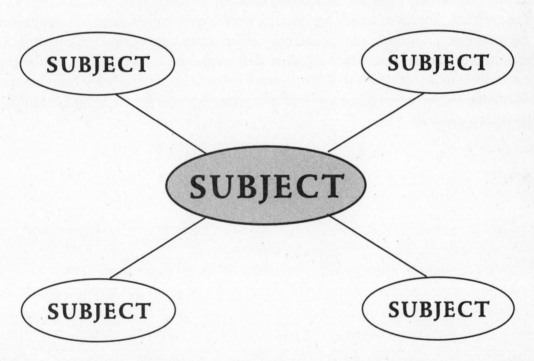

This approach offers a comfortable starting point for many teachers. The model focuses on one subject, and uses the content, skills, and insights of other subjects to extend the learning. The subject being investigated is broadened, students' knowledge is enriched, and skills in the other subject areas are solidified through learning opportunities that revisit previous learning. Many teachers are already making these kinds of connections in their programs.

Model 2: Interdisciplinary

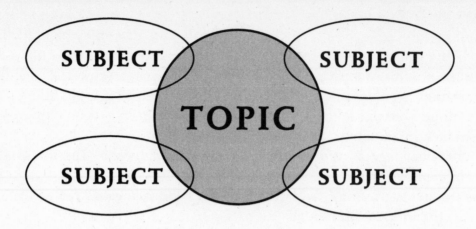

The most common attempt to move away from a single subject approach (Model 1: Subject-Based) involves the identification of a topic or issue to which other subjects might contribute. Topics or issues are usually more open-ended rather than subject specific, for example, environmental problems, self-identity, and conflict. Opportunities for meaningful integration of subjects are provided while the integrity of the subject disciplines is maintained. Although this model may be used successfully by individual teachers, it is most effective when a team of teachers pools its expertise to design and implement the classroom program.

Model 3: Transdisciplinary

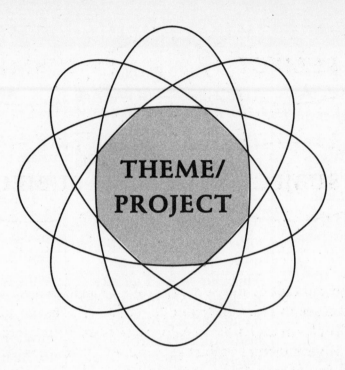

This model is based on connections across subject disciplines. Instead of asking what each subject can contribute to a central theme, teachers seek to identify important concepts or essential learnings related to a theme. The curriculum is shaped by students' needs, interests, and previous experience, and results in relevant and meaningful connections between education and the world beyond the school. The unit of study draws on a wide range of subject areas: the focus is the theme and how it will be developed. Content and skills are not abandoned but are placed within a context of meaning, which contributes to the likelihood that they will be learned.

Integration Delivery Models: Three Situations

ONE TEACHER — ONE CLASSROOM

An individual teacher may teach one subject to a class or, in a core situation, be responsible for the delivery of several subjects. In either case, many teachers now take advantage of various models to integrate the curriculum in their classrooms.

Integration Features

- requires no timetable changes
- occurs within the subject and course contexts in which the teacher is already comfortable and knowledgeable
- maintains the integrity of individual subjects, yet allows for the exploration of natural linkages among two or more subjects
- allows students to begin to make connections among subject areas in relation to their personal experiences

TWO PLUS TEACHERS — SEPARATE CLASSROOMS

The distinguishing feature of this model is the collaboration that takes place between two or more teachers. The delivery, however, occurs in individual classrooms. This allows for a variety of approaches to meet the needs and interests of both students and teachers.

Integration Features

- is facilitated by timetable adjustments allowing common planning time
- allows teachers to share their expertise and experience in planning together
- enhances the exploration of common elements within a variety of subject areas
- allows students to explore significant themes across a variety of subjects

TEAM PLANNING AND DELIVERY

This model brings together two or more teachers who share their respective subject disciplines to facilitate the investigation of a topic, theme, or issue. This involves collaborative planning, creative timetabling, and team teaching/delivery. This approach is particularly appropriate for developing themes relevant to the four subject clusters identified previously (page 8).

Integration Features

- requires common planning time as well as blocks of delivery time
- allows for creativity and flexibility in the planning and delivery of the program
- enables students to make vital links among disciplines by relating issues to the world beyond the classroom
- encourages students to assume ownership for their learning as teachers adopt the role of facilitators

Integration: The Process of Change

As teachers and administrators begin to plan for curriculum integration, they need to be aware of the phases of change indicated below.

PHASE 1

Teachers
- Review existing program
- Celebrate what's good:
  - teaching strategies
  - choice of content
  - evaluation techniques
- Identify what needs to be changed, focusing on learners' needs and interests, and learning styles
- Try something new – it's OK to be less than perfect
- Start small with something manageable
- Remember change builds on many small successes

PHASE 1

Administrator
- Help create a nurturing, collaborative climate
- Encourage and guide staff through systematic program review
- Remember the change continuum
- Encourage sharing among teachers informally or in team/subject clusters
- Provide staff in service and/or resources on the young adolescent
- At a school level determine how to meet the needs of early adolescents
- Involve students in setting school expectations
- Encourage extra-curricular activities, teacher-student contact outside classroom
- Stress that it's OK not to be perfect and to learn from mistakes

PHASE 2

- Find a person with whom to work
- Be willing to share and accept each other's ideas
- Focus on reasons, expectations with respect to collaboration
- Move slowly, keep it simple
- Keep the collaboration and sharing process positive and encouraging
- Persevere, even when the rules of the game keep changing

PHASE 2

- Provide time for talking and planning on a regular basis
- Be aware of interpersonal relationships ("Know Your Staff")
- Encourage risk-taking
- Offer support and encouragement as teachers move along the continuum
- Recognize that change is a complex process
- Give it lots of time

PHASE 3

- Be flexible with the timetable
- Accept the possibility of an increase in activity and noise level of students
- Remember that effective group skills require that students understand and apply the dynamics of group learning
- Choose topics that are relevant to the early adolescent to enhance motivation and commitment to the task
- Share the work load

PHASE 3

- Be flexible, creative, and supportive with timetable and space requirements
- Encourage the involvement of other staff members, i.e., teacher-librarian, physical education staff, Guidance/ Student Services staff
- Be involved and visible
- Remember that bottom-up planning is more effective than top-down
- Negotiate and be collaborative during the process
- Be available for consultation and intervention, guidance and support as needed or requested
- Be prepared to field questions or concerns from the community
- Be generous to staff — compliments are important and welcome

Sample Outlines

The following section provides information for teachers who want to design and develop integrated units. These sample unit outlines cover the steps involved in designing such units. The samples themselves should not be viewed as complete units; most offer only basic information and will need to be expanded by the teacher. Within the sample outlines the following headings have been used:

Rationale	This section describes the link between the Learning Outcomes and the student's relationship to the world outside the classroom.
Cross-Curricular Learnings	These are not all-inclusive; however, examples are provided of cross-curricular learnings which can be incorporated into the learning process.
Learning Outcomes	These are generated from the outcomes statements described in the curriculum.
Teacher Planning	This heading offers specific points to consider in designing and delivering a unit.
Sample Activities	Under this heading are suggested strategies through which knowledge, skills, and values are learned. These activities are based on the outcomes identified in each sample outline.
Evaluation	This section provides practical suggestions for assessing the effectiveness of the learning process. Pages 95 – 123 of this book provide examples of evaluation strategies and instruments that can be used in any unit.
Resources	Each educational authority has a wealth of support documents that can be used in conjunction with this book.

In each of the nine sample units, a different heading has been highlighted and expanded upon as indicated below:

Rationale (turn to pp. 45, 83)

Cross-Curricular Learnings (turn to pp. 26 – 27, 37 – 39, 57 – 61, 83)

Learning Outcomes (turn to pp. 45, 51, 63)

Teacher Planning (turn to pp. 27 – 28, 51 – 53, 69 – 70, 77 – 78)

Sample Activities (turn to pp. 57 – 60, 70 – 71, 74 – 75)

Evaluation (turn to pp. 29, 32 – 35, 39 – 43, 54)

Resources (turn to pp. 50, 56, 61, 81)

1

ONE TEACHER ONE CLASSROOM

An individual teacher may teach one subject to a class or, in a core situation, be responsible for the delivery of several subjects. In either case, many teachers now take advantage of various models to integrate the curriculum in their classrooms.

MODEL 1: SUBJECT-BASED
History

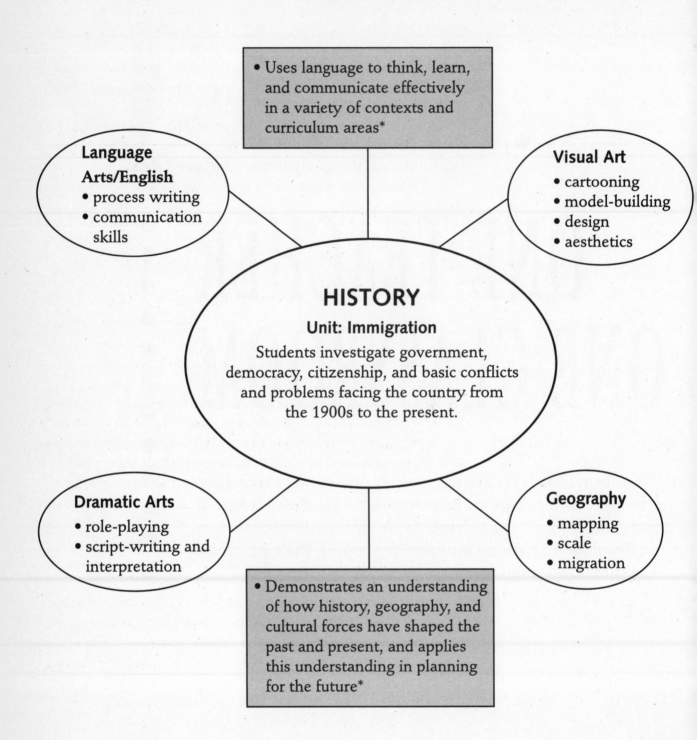

• Uses language to think, learn, and communicate effectively in a variety of contexts and curriculum areas*

Language Arts/English
• process writing
• communication skills

Visual Art
• cartooning
• model-building
• design
• aesthetics

HISTORY

Unit: Immigration

Students investigate government, democracy, citizenship, and basic conflicts and problems facing the country from the 1900s to the present.

Dramatic Arts
• role-playing
• script-writing and interpretation

Geography
• mapping
• scale
• migration

• Demonstrates an understanding of how history, geography, and cultural forces have shaped the past and present, and applies this understanding in planning for the future*

*The shaded statements show cross-curricular learnings and suggest how they could be incorporated into the sample unit.

| Rationale | Through an examination and discussion of the problems of the immigrants who came to a new country in the 1900s, students will understand the hardship and conflict involved in facing a new environment. |

Learning Outcomes

Learners will:
- identify, analyze, and evaluate information about the immigrant experience
- identify and appreciate the hardships and struggles of these people
- compare and contrast past and present lifestyles (1900s and today)
- demonstrate the ability to synthesize and create an aesthetically pleasing product incorporating new knowledge.

Teacher Planning

This sample unit would be applicable to core teachers responsible for the delivery of two or more subject areas which include History and Language Arts. An integration of Visual Arts and Dramatic Arts is also included.

- This unit provides an opportunity for informal collaboration with other teachers regarding integration of subject matter. Contributions from teachers responsible for other subjects is encouraged with regard to resources and expertise.
- Throughout this unit, the teacher is primarily a resource person working to facilitate the learning process. This role includes monitoring student progress, responding to individual and group needs, keeping students on task, and guiding those students in need of additional skill development and knowledge.
- Teachers are encouraged to make available a variety of resources for student use; the teacher-librarian may be consulted for help in this area. Classroom resources would ideally include a variety of print resources, pictures, slides, filmstrips, audio-cassettes, a computer data base, building materials, art paper, markers, coloured pencils, information sheets, and so forth.
- Resources may vary depending on the student-selected activities.
- Both students and teacher will find it convenient if students can have access to a work space where pertinent information or materials are available.

- Sharing of final products with the class would help to ensure that all students are exposed to a common knowledge base and have an opportunity to demonstrate learning outcomes.
- Sample activities in this unit lend themselves to small group and/or individual learning situations. Student desks could be arranged in groups to permit easy transition from one activity to the next as well as for sharing and peer teaching.
- One area of the room could be designated as the area for any hands-on or building activities. A larger space may be needed for the extended activities. These might include:
  - hallways
  - art room
  - drama area
  - gymnasium
  - cafeteria
- Suggested time allotment for completion of this unit is three to four weeks. Though activities may be limited to 40-minute blocks of time, longer time blocks would be beneficial if scheduling allows.
- A half or full day could be set aside for whole class activities chosen from the suggested Extension Activities (p. 31).

Sample Activities

The sample activities which begin on page 30 encompass a wide variety of learning styles and product presentation. Background information on immigrant history and the position of the government with respect to the influx of immigrants in the 1900s should be provided by the teacher before students attempt the Sample Activities included in this unit.

Students may be given the opportunity to modify any of the activities below and may also be encouraged to develop their own activity and/or final product. Changes should be fully discussed with the teacher before the student proceeds.

Evaluation   Student contributions to the evaluation process may be incorporated into this unit. Individual and/or class discussion should elicit a variety of assessment and evaluation criteria that are agreeable to students. Assessment and evaluation strategies should include self, peer, and teacher instruments. On pages 32 – 35 are examples of specific evaluation techniques that may be used.

Resources   • Local educational authority support documents
  • *Integrated Programs for Adolescents*, page 90 (Pembroke, 1993).
  • *A Pioneer Story*, Barbara Greenwood (Kids Can Press, 1994).

THE IMMIGRANTS: SAMPLE ACTIVITIES

Instructions to Students

Choose two (2) of the following activities to complete based on your knowledge and research of immigrants in the 1900s.

1. You are the member of a family that has immigrated in the 1900s. Using a questionnaire developed in class, interview family members about their journey to this country. Share this information with the class.
2. You have decided to help others coming to settle here. Write an instruction booklet outlining the procedures for building a home. Be certain that each step is clear and accompanied by a labelled diagram.
3. Write a letter to your cousin in England, describing all the things the native inhabitants have taught you which have helped you adapt and survive in your new home. Use descriptive language and work with a partner to revise and proofread your letter.
4. Examine the types of occupations that the immigrants brought to their new country. Prepare a newspaper ad for specific occupations needed in the 1900s. Write a resumé from a newcomer applying to fill one of these positions.
5. In comic strip form, compare the lives of teachers and students then to the lives of teachers and students today.
6. Dramatize a family discussing their reasons for leaving their homeland, their expectations about their new home, the hardships faced, feelings of homesickness, and reasons why they have chosen to stay in their new country.
7. You have opened a general store in town. Prepare a poster of the times to be placed in your store window advertising the items you will offer and their prices.
8. Design a portfolio that contains a variety of artifacts which describe or show people today what life was like for your family. Items you may consider once are:
   - floor plan or model of a home
   - furniture samples or design
   - articles of clothing
   - tools
   - food
   - games and toys
   - musical instruments or sheet music for popular songs
9. Why would anyone put up with all these hardships? Create a poster that outlines all the reasons why someone would want to be an immigrant.
10. Create a "Trader's Guide" of transportation vehicles owned by the newcomers. Be sure to include both a description and an outline of the advantages for each type of transportation as well as an illustration.

11. Read a novel that deals with the immigrant experience and respond to it through a creative medium (poem, video, role play, drawing, board game) or rewrite a part of the novel (for example, change a scene or add a new character).
12. Keep a journal account of your trip to the new country. Include in your entries: anecdotes, feelings, impressions, descriptions of landforms, interesting locations, climate changes, scenery, wildlife, how you planned your trip, and any other category you can think of.

Extension Activities

Additional whole class activities could also be incorporated using this model. A few suggestions follow:

1. Create a class newspaper from the 1900s.
2. On large pieces of craft paper design a mural depicting your life as an immigrant. Include a variety of visuals, such as a map showing the routes you travelled and illustrations of clothing, social activities, or farming activities.
3. Design and create a 3-D model of a new settlement.
4. Plan a 1900s Day. Dress in period clothes and present a variety of skits, displays, booths (for example, a food sampling booth), or games. Invite teachers, other students, and parents to participate.

Final Product Evaluation Sheet

Note: The Final Product Evaluation sheet (below and p. 33) is the result of student-teacher negotiation. In order to give students ownership in the learning process, the five areas to be evaluated are agreed upon as a class, with teacher guidance. Through discussion, the weighting for each of the five areas is determined, resulting in a flexible mark range for each. Learners then specify the value they want to give each section based on their own learning styles, effort, interests, and talents. The total must match a predetermined maximum (such as 100 or 150 marks). The teacher then uses each learner's decisions as the basis for evaluation. This type of evaluation enhances learners' awareness of how they learn. Teachers could also use this evaluation sheet to allow learners to evaluate themselves. Two samples have been included. One has been filled in, showing how a teacher and students might wish to allocate the mark ranges. The other is blank.

Final Product Evaluation Sheet

Topic: THE IMMIGRANTS

Teacher-Generated Mark Based on Student Selected Ranges

Activity Selected:

1. Research Skills
   Primary/Secondary Sources
   Negotiated Mark Range   10 – 20   /15

2. Organization/Clarity
   Negotiated Mark Range   15 – 25   /20

3. Originality/Creativity
   Negotiated Mark Range   15 – 30   /15

4. Content/ Written Work
   Accuracy, Factual Content
   Negotiated Mark Range   20 – 35   /20

5. Final Product Presentation
   Overall Impression, Cohesiveness, Polish
   Negotiated Mark Range   25 – 35   /30

Final Mark   */100*

Final Product Evaluation Sheet

Topic:

© *Getting It All Together*, Pembroke Publishers.
Teachers who purchase this book have permission to copy for classroom use.

Teacher-Generated Mark
Based on Student
Selected Ranges

Activity Selected:

1. Research Skills
   Primary/Secondary Sources
   Negotiated Mark Range

2. Organization/Clarity
   Negotiated Mark Range

3. Originality/Creativity
   Negotiated Mark Range

4. Content/ Written Work
   Accuracy, Factual Content
   Negotiated Mark Range

5. Final Product Presentation
   Overall Impression, Cohesiveness, Polish
   Negotiated Mark Range

Final Mark

Peer Evaluation

STUDENT PRESENTATION: _____

DATE: _____

1. List three things you learned from the final product.

   _____

   _____

   _____

2. How did this final product display knowledge of immigration history?

3. How did this final product demonstrate creativity?

4. Suggest how this final product could be improved.

5. What aspects of the life of immigrants would you now like to learn more about?

Tracking/Monitoring Checklist: Immigration Unit

STUDENT NAME	Works independently	Exhibits task commitment	Meets deadlines	Uses a variety of resources	Understands process	Incorporates unique and creative ideas	Understands key concepts	Shares expertise with peers	Cooperates in group setting	Displays organizational abilities	Includes detail	Accepts help and guidance	Overall work ethic and commitment		

MODEL 2: INTERDISCIPLINARY
Investigations

Mathematics

Organization and representation of data
- develop problem-solving skills
- collect, record, display, and interpret data

Science

Problem-solving and data representation
- use scientific processes to investigate living things and solve problems
- collect and analyze data using charts and graphs to demonstrate results

INVESTIGATIONS

- a variety of process models (e.g., inquiry model, problem-solving model, scientific methods)
- investigations are related to specific curriculum content
- open-ended procedures and outcomes

Media

Media literacy:
- identify, interpret, and experience a variety of techniques used to create and sell products through many media

Geography

Investigation of an issue
- design suitable questions focusing on changes to be made or a problem to be solved
- develop a visual organizer for gathering information to answer question(s)

Rationale   Students need to know how to make effective decisions and solve problems using appropriate investigative techniques in order to become capable, independent learners. Because different subjects provide varied yet interrelated approaches to these investigations, students need the opportunity to practise these skills in a variety of contexts and to become aware of the common elements they possess.

Learning Outcomes   Learners will:
- use the critical and creative thinking models that are characteristic of each subject to formulate and solve problems, make decisions, visualize, and create solutions
- demonstrate understanding of the similarities and differences among the different models and skills used for problem-solving and decision-making in the various subject areas
- demonstrate understanding of the meaning of print and other symbol systems
- be able to understand and make informed judgments about the value of print and other symbol systems or media.

Teacher Planning   In this sample, the teacher is responsible for Language Arts/ English, Mathematics, Geography, and Science. Using language to think, learn, and communicate effectively is a cross-curricular learning for all subjects. This sample will model this learning in the four subject areas. However, the approach is equally valid in other subjects.

   Although there are several possible ways to approach this topic, teachers are encouraged to use an integrated approach that conducts the investigation in each subject at the same time.

- Review the various investigation models as outlined for each of the subjects involved (see **Resources** section, p. 39).
- Because comparison of the various investigation models involves abstract reasoning, the teacher is advised to make this comparison only incidentally or at opportune moments.
- Decide which units in each subject are best suited for this exercise. Possible areas of study are included in the sample activities below.
- Timetable the units selected in such a way that integration can occur.

- The time allocation will vary depending on the pre-skill level of the students and the specific problems selected in each subject.
- The time allocation for each subject need not be equal, but should be simultaneous to facilitate comparisons.
- The learning activities used in this approach will dictate the space requirements.

Sample Activities

Mathematics

1. Have students solve a wide variety of word problems or puzzles.

Science

1. Use simple experiments to review scientific method(s). Provide some experiments.
2. In groups, have students create questions for a student survey about fashions, favourite foods, favourite music stars, or any other relevant category, and chart the results.

Geography

1. Ask students to follow a procedure to bring about an improvement in community or school life, such as the curtailing of littering, by determining:
   - whether there is a problem
   - who is affected
   - what the cause is
   - what steps could be taken to correct the problem
   After a period of time, determine whether the plan was successful.
2. Choose an activity:
   - Design a traffic survey.
   - Calculate population density for your local school community.
   - Create a school census questionnaire.

Media Literacy

1. Have students choose an item advertised in the media, and investigate how competing companies advertise their products. What are the similarities and differences? What is the "hook"? What influence do these different angles have on people as consumers?
2. Ask students to keep a log of the products advertised on television throughout the day and record this data in chart or graph form. Sample headings might include: Type of Product, Length of Commercial, Number of Commercials, Prime Time, Soaps, and Talk Shows.

Students could also examine and discuss the way in which types of commercials change throughout the day. Why do advertisers prefer certain time slots for their products?

Evaluation   Students could identify or create a problem requiring the contribution of one subject area for solution. As an extension, students could be encouraged to use other investigative models. See also the evaluation strategies suggested on pp. 40 – 43.

Example: Working in small groups, students identify a real-life issue of interest to them which they will investigate using an appropriate model (see **Sample Activities** section, pp. 38 – 39). Working in consultation with one or more teachers, the students will design an organizational framework or rubric for the investigation. A sample rubric appears on pp. 40 – 42.

> Note: Throughout this activity, the emphasis is placed on the process of investigation and not just on the final product. For that reason, the students need to work through the process of developing their own organizational framework that is unique to their particular investigation.
>
> Based on the organizational framework, the students and teacher(s) establish the criteria for evaluation of the investigation. If appropriate, an outside evaluator with expertise in the field of investigation could be involved in establishing criteria and in the evaluation process itself.

Resources   • *Integrated Programs for Adolescents*, Hazardous Waste Unit, page 58 (Pembroke, 1993).

• Curriculum documents from your own educational authority.

Sample Rubric

STUDENTS: _____

PROBLEM/ISSUE/CONCERN: _____

_____

_____

1. What do we know now about the problem/issue/concern?

_____

_____

_____

_____

2. What do we need to know about the problem/issue/concern?

_____

_____

_____

_____

3. What investigative model is best suited to this investigation?

_____

_____

_____

4. What sources of information (both human and physical) should we consult as part of our research?

_____

_____

_____

_____

5. What does our research suggest are possible solutions?

_____

_____

_____

_____

6. What are the implications/consequences for each possible solution?

_____

_____

_____

_____

7. Based on our investigations, we recommend the following solution for these reasons:

SOLUTION: _____

_____

_____

REASONS: 1. _____

2. _____

3. _____

8. Who should our recommendations be presented to? Why?

_____

_____

_____

9. How can we best present our recommendations to this target audience?

_____

_____

_____

10. What criteria are most appropriate for evaluating this investigation? Why?

_____

_____

_____

11. Who should be involved in this evaluation process? Why?

_____

_____

_____

Sample Criteria for Evaluation

STUDENTS: _____

INVESTIGATION: _____

On a scale of 1 (low) to 5 (high), evaluate the investigation on each of the following:

1. Clear description of the problem/issue/concern	1	2	3	4	5
2. Brainstorming re: problem/issue/concern	1	2	3	4	5
3. Appropriate investigative model selected	1	2	3	4	5
4. Researching the problem	1	2	3	4	5
5. Exploration of alternative solutions	1	2	3	4	5
6. Analysis of implications for solutions	1	2	3	4	5
7. Justification for proposed solution	1	2	3	4	5
8. Presentation of recommendations	1	2	3	4	5

Comments: _____

_____

_____

_____

Evaluator(s): _____

_____

_____

MODEL 3: TRANSDISCIPLINARY
Citizenship

- examine the process of becoming a citizen
- explore the rights and responsibilities of citizenship, the unique features of this country and its population, and aspects of government
- describe what being a citizen means
- demonstrate good citizenship through community involvement

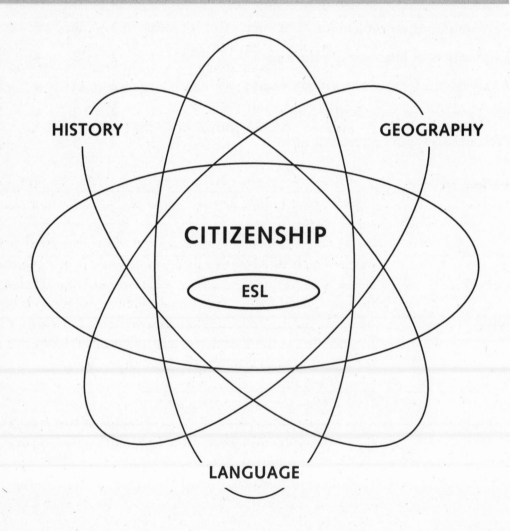

| Rationale | This sample is designed to help learners acquire a sense of pride and responsibility toward their school, community, and country and to understand the contributions they can make to the society and culture. Students require personal experiences to help them understand and become involved in the practices of citizenship. Opportunities should be provided for learners to develop leadership skills by direct participation in the school and in the wider community. The theme of citizenship has been identified as relevant to the needs and interests of the learners since a number of them are on their way to becoming citizens. |

Learning Outcomes

Learners will:
- recognize the importance of, and participate actively in, their families, school, and community
- work cooperatively on common tasks in school and in the community
- demonstrate their respect for this country and its democratic and pluralistic traditions
- appreciate the rights and responsibilities of individuals as citizens of the local community, of a country, and of the global community
- understand the contributions that immigrants have made to society.

Teacher Planning

In this sample, the teacher has a withdrawal program for second-language learners. They are also integrated in other classrooms where appropriate.

The teacher is planning to include a variety of theme aspects which will involve learners actively in the planning and delivery of the unit. The unit will have both a school and community-based focus, and will provide learners with a number of opportunities for hands-on experiences. As a culminating activity, the teacher and learners will work together to arrange for a Citizenship Court to be held in the school.

The theme will include:
- aspects of government
- key elements of the geography of the country
- leadership development focusing on community involvement using language for content-based instruction.
- Teachers could consult with other staff in the English, Geography, and History, departments for resources and expertise — this could become a joint planning activity. For example, all of the students

in the grade could be surveyed by Second Language learners regarding their country of origin, and the results graphed and displayed for the school.

- Appropriate materials for Second Language learners may be obtained from the government.
- When considering physical space requirements other than individual classrooms, teachers should plan on using a large area such as the auditorium or the gymnasium. Booking of space outside of the school could also figure into the planning for this unit.
- Since the theme is a major focus of the program, a significant block of time will be needed.
- **Note: A minimum of six months' lead time is needed for Citizenship Court requests. Apply in writing to the local office.**

Sample Activities

1. Working with the students, plan and make the necessary arrangements for the Citizenship Court. A variety of student leadership roles may be developed through this activity.
2. Develop and conduct a survey of students' countries of origin. Map the results and display for the school.
3. Working with the students, make a classroom display of maps and illustrations of various parts of this country to familiarize students with its physical and human diversity. Travel posters, pictures of different seasons, and regional occupations are good choices.
4. As a class, explore the rights and responsibilities of citizens, aspects of government, and the unique features of the country and its population. This investigation could be developed using the following questions:
   - What do you know?
   - What do you want to know?
   - What do you need to know?
   Language anthologies and videos or films which describe the immigrant experience assist learners in relating those experiences to their own experiences.
5. Have students write about or visually depict what being a citizen means to them. A few student presentations might be incorporated into the Citizenship Court ceremony.

6. Provide opportunities for students to plan and participate in a good citizenship project, such as:
   - organizing a food drive
   - working with seniors in the community
   - organizing an outdoor clean-up or beautification project

Evaluation In addition to using the evaluation strategies of the program, the teacher may wish to establish a balance between evaluating process and product, and use a variety of teacher-directed, student, self, and peer evaluation instruments (see pp. 96 – 123 for samples).

Resources • *E.S.L. Is Everybody's Business* (Pembroke, 1994).
   • Local educational authority guidelines.

TWO PLUS TEACHERS SEPARATE CLASSROOMS

The distinguishing feature of this model is the collaboration that takes place between two or more teachers. The delivery, however, occurs in individual classrooms. This allows for a variety of different approaches to meet the needs and interests of both students and teachers.

MODEL 1: SUBJECT-BASED
Science

FAMILY STUDIES
Families and the Global Food Supply
- impact on family of the availability of certain foods
- current food crises — causes/impacts
- technological advances related to food supply, e.g., dehydration, refrigeration, rapid transportation

Clothing as an Expression of Lifestyle
- physical and chemical characteristics of fibres
- fabrics that modify the impact of climate on the body
- ecological concerns
- textile production

VISUAL ARTS
Design
- interior decorators modify the environment with plants

History
- plants provide primitive forms of colour and paint

Drawing
- naturalistic representations in landscapes

SCIENCE
Importance of Plants
Plants are important not only in the biochemical processes which they carry on, but also in the many environmental functions they fulfill. A great number of economic activities depend on plants and their products.

GEOGRAPHY
Natural Resources of Canada
- useful products derived from plants
- fruit-growing: The Niagara Fruit Belt

Environmental Concerns
- lumbering and urbanization threaten areas of natural vegetation
- plants alter climate by providing shade and windbreaks

MATHEMATICS
Measurement and its applications
- apply concepts of perimeter and area to leaves
- coordinate Geometry and congruence transformations
- draw figures of leaves on a grid given the coordinates
- draw image of a figure on a grid under translation, reflection, and rotation
- apply rate, ratio, percent
- express the relationship of land use, agriculture, natural resources, urban growth

Rationale	Through teacher collaboration and simultaneous delivery of common elements in different subjects, students will participate in a less fragmented learning experience.
Learning Outcomes	Learners will:
Visual Arts	• demonstrate an appreciation of the contribution of plants to the history of painting and their influence on design and drawing
Geography	• demonstrate an understanding of the importance plants play in the economy and the environment and the relationship between natural and artificial environments
Family Studies	• demonstrate an appreciation of the role green plants play in the daily lives of the individual, the family, and the global community
Mathematics	• generate and interpret graphs and compare the suitability of different graphs for depicting data • identify and apply the properties of plane figures
Cross-Subject Projects	• appreciate the aesthetic qualities of natural and artificial environments • demonstrate an ability to apply aesthetic, scientific and mathematical concepts to the environment.
Teacher Planning	The dialogue that follows is meant to illustrate what might happen when two colleagues get together to talk about initiating an integrated unit. Suggestions for teachers to consider in their planning are:

- Be willing to examine curriculum for common or complementary components.
- Be open to suggestions from colleagues and students which may generate independent study projects (see Sample Projects, p. 54).
- Be flexible when it comes to timetable changes.
- Make students aware of objectives of the integrated program.
- Keep your sense of humour and persevere!

PLANNING AN INTERDISCIPLINARY UNIT

Barry is a Mathematics teacher and Mei Ling teaches Science. Both are experienced teachers and have been teaching their courses for a number of years. Faced with new directives from the local educational authority to provide an integrated approach to curriculum, they agree to explore the feasibility of integrating the curriculum in their different subjects. On another occasion, they had discussed the possibility of integrating the content of four or five subject areas. However, realizing the importance of "starting small," they now want to explore the possibilities offered by their two subject areas first.

Barry and Mei Ling: Where do we start?

Mei Ling: One of the problems will be that Science is more content-based than Mathematics. Yes, there are certain skills that are taught, but I'm also responsible for the students acquiring a certain amount of knowledge.

Barry: I agree, and another problem is that although we teach the same classes, they're not held at the same time and we're at completely opposite ends of the school, so team-teaching is out of the question.

Mei Ling: Those seem to be the two key obstacles, and there are probably others. I wonder if there's any way around them.

Barry: Maybe we should start by looking at our curriculum guidelines and cross-curricular learning outcomes. We want the students to be able to employ mathematical knowledge and skills to solve practical problems.

Mei Ling: Yes, and we also want them to evaluate relationships between humans and the environment and be concerned for living things. One of the core Science units is "Green Plants." We look at the parts and processes of a plant — we write equations for them and also talk about their importance in the environment. There are certainly connections with both Math and the Learning Outcomes.

Barry: You're right. It also seems to me that it might be possible to do something with the area and perimeter of leaves in my unit on measurement. The students could also use various leaf shapes in "Transformational Geometry." That would provide opportunities for using critical and creative thinking skills in a problem-solving situation. Don't you also do some tests or experiments? Could we could use the results for graphing?

Mei Ling: Yes, we do simple tests for starch and carbon dioxide which look at the processes and functions of plant parts. But the students could also do some graphing of how plants are used in society. You know, there are many plants in some parts of the school and none in others for different reasons. I know one teacher has them in the room to provide some moisture.

Barry: All right, we agree there are some common areas in the two subject areas. Maybe there are some connections with others. You mentioned how plants are placed throughout the school. The Visual Arts department does a unit on interior design, and plants are certainly used to modify both interior and exterior environments.

Mei Ling: Family Studies focuses on Global Food Supply and fabrics and fibres. There's definitely a link there with the "Green Plants" unit. Perhaps we've also missed one of the most obvious connections — plants as a natural resource in Geography.

Barry: I guess it's a start. At least if we look at coordinating the timing of units we already teach around a common focus, it will both reinforce the learning and move toward meeting educational expectations.

Mei Ling: This might work, but I think we need to talk some more. I guess over lunch again tomorrow is the only time, unless we have a common prep period. Bring your timetable with you and we'll keep our fingers crossed! There's the bell, I have to run!

Barry: I'll invite Farouk from Visual Arts. Why don't you approach Kaz from Family Studies and Sue from the Geography department?

Mei Ling: Good idea! See you tomorrow.

- The time allotment should be appropriate to individual subjects and guidelines. The time does not have to be equal in all subjects but delivery should be simultaneous and of comparable duration.

• Students could modify an exterior or interior space through the use of green plants, taking into consideration:
  • the suitability of various plants for that environment, e.g., soil, light, water, and temperature requirements
  • the function of the space
  • the contribution of plants to aesthetics, e.g., shape, height, colour, texture
  • safety
• Students could investigate the extent to which another society in the world makes use of green plants, e.g., food, shelter, clothing, art.
• Students could use the shape of a leaf and computer graphics software to create a pattern that might be incorporated into a fabric, wallpaper or ceramics design.

Evaluation

Evaluation should be based on the Learning Outcomes noted above. Teachers may wish to include observation strategies. See the Evaluation section, pp. 95 – 123, for the following observation instruments:

Anecdotal Comment Sheet, p. 98
Checklist (Tracking/monitoring), p. 100

As students become involved in independent projects, teachers may wish to include the following evaluation instruments also found in the Evaluation section.

Conference Record Sheet p. 110
Self-Evaluation Sheet p. 112
Peer Evaluation Sheet p. 115
Final Product Evaluation Sheet p. 32
Evaluation of Another Group's Presentation p. 116

Resources   Local educational authority guidelines
for: Science
Geography
Visual Arts
Family Studies

MODEL 2: INTERDISCIPLINARY
Technological Competence

LANGUAGE

Novel Studies
Discussion of literature should focus on personal responses to themes and ideas rather than analysis.

Media Literacy
Television has turned out to be one of the most phenomenal of all human inventions. It touches lives more intimately and pervasively than anything that predates it with the possible exception of the discovery of fire.

HISTORY

Unit 3: The Nation Expands
Unit 4: A Changing Society

TECHNOLOGICAL COMPETENCE

In becoming technologically competent, students learn to create and use technologies, evaluate their social impact, and promote the responsible use of technologies.

MUSIC

Understanding the role and importance of technology in music through listening, performing, and composing.

DESIGN TECHNOLOGY

Students should be given opportunities to recognize the design procedure as a sequence for developing and completing projects in a self-directed manner.

Rationale   In this sample, technological knowledge and perspective, one of the cross-curricular outcomes, is highlighted within the curriculum expectations of the four subjects. Students will have opportunities to create and use technology, as well as evaluate its impact on society in a variety of subject areas.

The unique needs of adolescents are met through opportunities to interact with their peers, take ownership for their learning, and make connections between their personal experiences and interests, and the curriculum.

Learning Outcomes   Learners will:
- demonstrate competence in using and evaluating a variety of technologies
- recognize technological concepts and applications in the home, school, and community
- recognize the impact of technological change on their personal lives and society through time.

Teacher Planning   Teachers are advised to approach at least one colleague from another subject discipline with whom to collaborate. Then:
- As a team decide on the number and scope of activities from which the students might choose.
- Determine the amount of time required for the completion of the activities; this will vary depending on the type of the activity.
- Be aware that timetable changes may be necessary to accommodate the joint delivery of the unit by individual teachers.
- Make students aware of the objectives of the integrated program.
- Be open to suggested modified or additional activities and projects from colleagues and students.
- Arrange for "special" teaching areas if they are required.

The amount of time needed will vary depending on the activities chosen. However, it is essential that these be undertaken simultaneously and the time allotment be predetermined by the teachers involved.

Sample Activities

History   1. Have students design and build a model to show how engineers used technology to solve problems during the construction of the railway in one of the geographic regions it crossed.

2. Students could depict the working conditions in an industry of the late 19th century through drama.
3. Students could research one improvement that was made in a late 19th-century industry and design a poster advertising the resulting advantages.

Language

The following novels by Bill Freeman, all published by Formac Publishing Company, are suggested:

> *The Shantymen of Cache Lake*
> *The Last Voyage of the Scotian*
> *Danger on the Tracks*

After reading the novel(s), students may do the following:
1. Research and role play a character associated with the technology of the time, e.g., ship's captain, lumberman, railway engineer. This activity could be extended by combining these performances into a "Living Museum," complete with costumes, mini-sets, and music.
2. Assume the identity of a character and write a diary entry describing his/her feelings about the benefits and risks of the technological changes in the story.
3. As an employer, write a want ad for a job in a business of the time. Emphasize the technological skills the successful applicant will require.

Other Resources

- Patricia & Frederick McKessack, *A Long Hard Journey: The Story of the Pullman Porter.* New York, NY: Walker & Co.

- William Wormser, *The Iron Horse: How the Railroads Changed America.* New York, NY: Walker & Co.

Media Literacy

TELEVISION FAMILIES

The following activities encourage students to evaluate the influence of television technology on their views of society and the world.

With the students, brainstorm the titles of some of the television programs that portray families, then do the following:
1. Compare the behaviours of various members of the television families with the behaviours of people in real life.
2. Use role-playing to show ways in which these people treat each other in conflict situations and interact with each other in non-crisis situations.

3. Through role-playing or discussion, compare the above television scenes with real-life behaviours.
4. Discuss the ways the television parents are portrayed compared with real-life parents.
5. Discuss things students may have wanted to alter in their own life because of what has been seen on these shows.
6. Compare how students' and the lives of their family members would be different if they were to imitate a television family for twenty-four hours.

TELEVISION FANTASY AND REALITY

The above activities, based on the familiar world of the family, were designed to help students distinguish real-life experience from the constructed views of television. The following activities both summarize and extend this perspective.

1. Brainstorm the groups or individuals who are currently featured on television (e.g., police, private detectives, teachers, doctors, single parents).
2. Form small groups to choose a suitable television group or individual to study. Compare these television images with real-life experiences and try to offer explanations for any discrepancy between them.

Examples:

SUBJECT(S)	TV IMAGE	REAL LIFE	EXPLANATION
Police	Pursuit of criminals in fast chases	routine tasks (e.g., speeding tickets)	In entertainment, we prefer to see the glamorous and the exciting as opposed to the commonplace.

TELEVISION CHARACTERS

1. Select one of your favourite television characters and explore that character in depth.
   a) Have you ever known anyone like that character?
   b) Is it possible for such a person to exist in real life? Explain.
2. Choose a method to depict a visit by one of your favourite characters to the classroom or your home (e.g., poem, short story, role-playing, comic strip).

Music

1. Students could use recorded sample sounds to complement a photograph or painting.
2. Ask students to identify how a composer chooses instruments which enhance the theme or mood of a movie or TV show.
3. Students could use a synthesizer to create a rhythm composition combining built-in and original patterns.
4. Have students identify the influences of rock videos on their self-presentation (e.g., hair and clothing styles). Why do we find large numbers of "clones" of popular rock stars?
5. Rock stars cultivate or fabricate an elaborate stage *persona*, reinforced by costumes and technical effects and enhanced by media hype. Have students brainstorm a list of the myths, qualities, and values associated with two or three of the most popular rock stars. Discuss with the class the reason for each *persona* and its effects on the audience.

Design Technology

1. Have students apply the design procedure to improve an existing product, toy, or tool.
2. Students could design a product that would be useful in the home, e.g., grooming accessory organizer, or a product that would fulfill a school need, e.g., keyboard cover for a computer.

Evaluation

It is crucial that evaluation practices focus on the outcomes related to Technological Competence, i.e, creating/using technology, evaluating its impact on society, and promoting its use. Evidence of these outcomes will vary depending on the subject and the nature of the activity or project. Students may be asked to identify unique and common elements relating to technological competence in the activities.

For observation sheets and work samples, see pp. 97 – 101.

Resources
- Historical novels that complement the history and language units
- Local educational authority guidelines for:
  Media Literacy
  History
  Design Technology
  Music
  Language

Teachers should also try to locate equipment appropriate to the selected activities, such as a synthesizer, tape recorders, or television.

MODEL 3: TRANSDISCIPLINARY
Patterns

PATTERNS
- recognizing
- identifying
- duplicating
- creating

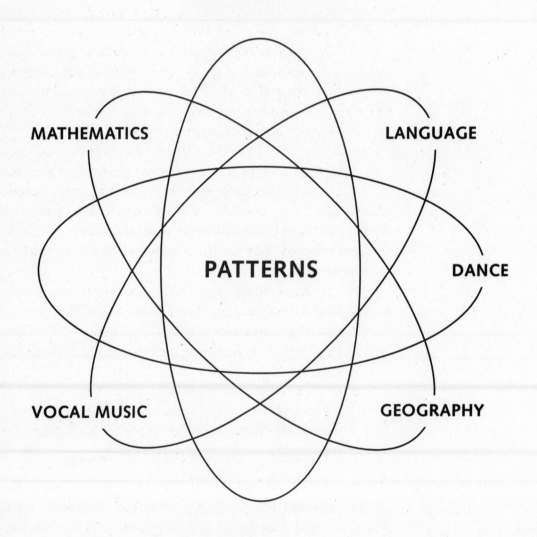

MATHEMATICS

LANGUAGE

DANCE

PATTERNS

VOCAL MUSIC

GEOGRAPHY

Rationale   This thematic unit draws from and extends the concept of patterns found in all areas of the curriculum. Recognizing, identifying, duplicating, and creating patterns through an integrated approach offers a meaningful learning opportunity to the adolescent. As the learner uses these skills, a broad-based view of patterns within the environment is gradually developed.

Learning Outcomes   Learning outcomes are observable and measurable knowledge, skills, and values that students are expected to have acquired and developed at certain key stages of their schooling. They describe what students should know, should be able to do, and should value as a result of their learning experiences.

For example, if the aim of learning is to enable all learners to become competent communicators, we must develop and provide classroom program opportunities which will produce this effect and allow it to be measured and demonstrated.

Within a unit, course or program, learning outcomes will address the knowledge, skills, and values which learners need to demonstrate that the outcome has been achieved. It is important to have a balance between the knowledge, skills, and values — at times, one or other of these areas will be emphasized more than the others. However, within the whole program a balance of the three areas must be achieved.

Outcomes also have a hierarchy in that they proceed from the simple to the complex. In this sample, the outcomes have been organized to demonstrate this increasing complexity and to indicate which of the three aspects have been addressed.

Learners will:
- recognize, identify, and describe patterns as they appear in the environment (knowledge and skill)
- recognize and describe the similarities and differences in patterns throughout the curriculum (knowledge and skill)
- demonstrate and appreciate an understanding of the elements of patterns (knowledge and values)
- demonstrate an ability to duplicate and create original patterns in a variety of forms (skill).

Teacher Planning   Although this unit is infused with the content and skills from different curriculum areas, the sample activities are a stepping stone toward developing a more global perspective. Teachers collaborating on this unit might choose aspects of the theme as their focal point. Delivery of the activities may be done individually or as a team to separate classes, combined classes, or mixed groupings as the subject disciplines are blended and are no longer viewed as distinct and isolated entities in the timetable.

Teachers are advised to:
- gather resources: subject guidelines, "coffee-table" books, aerial maps/photographs, list of possible field trip destinations and guest speakers
- choose specific focuses as a team within the theme of patterns
- be aware that the timetable should reflect large blocks of time which might be called Integrated Studies
- build in student contributions in the planning, delivery, and evaluation of the theme and its components
- plan for a common space to be set up as an exhibit area which ties the work of several classes together
- arrange for physical spaces other than the classroom, such as the library, cafeteria, or gymnasium
- realize that the time required will vary with the depth and breadth of the activities chosen.

Sample Activities

1. Ask students to read several examples of a type of poetry. Have the students identify the patterns, e.g., rhyme scheme, meter, common themes, and use these as a basis for creating their own poetry.
2. As a class, gather examples of children's verse from around the world. Share these with other class members, identifying the patterns within, e.g., number of lines, rhyme scheme, repetition, content.
3. Have students write a modern-day version of one of the poems located in Activity 2 based on the patterns found. Students could illustrate the verses and include them in a published class collection.
4. Ask students to identify the patterns in the images of males and females presented in advertisements. For example:
   - what activities are they involved in?
   - who is in the foreground/background?
   - who is active/passive?
   - what is their body language?

   Ask students to create their own advertisements that break the pattern.
5. Introduce patterns that appear in musical form(s), e.g., stanza, refrain, rondo. Using the lyrics of selected pieces of popular music, have students identify and compare the patterns they discover.

6. In small groups, have students create a rhythmic or melodic short, repeated pattern (ostanato) as an accompaniment to a piece of poetry. Students could tape their creations.

7. Ask students to compare the rhythm in a variety of musical styles, e.g., waltz, march, polka, calypso. Students could use body parts, instruments, or classroom materials to reproduce like rhythms.

8. Have students create a series of movements that capture a variety of rhythms suggested by the music.

9. Students could use concrete materials and graph/dot paper to experiment with flips, slides, turns, and so forth.

10. Encourage the students to do some reading about M.C. Escher and his tessellating drawings. Students could choose a tessellating figure, design a plane tessellation, and colour it. On a piece of cartridge paper, students could design an "Escher-type" drawing.

11. As a class, use aerial maps to identify and compare the planning and layout of roads in urban and suburban settings. Formulate criteria city planners consider when designing transportation routes.

12. Students could plan and draw a map illustrating a new city, indicating different transportation route patterns. Encourage students to be creative and able to defend their decisions.

13. Plan a field trip to a shopping area, plaza, or mall. Students could observe and record the patterns of store locations, formulate reasons for store placement, and design their own shopping area using patterns to attract a specific clientele or market segment.

14. As a class, create a scrapbook of photographs or sketches illustrating the wide variety of patterns in the environment.

15. Arrange to have an interior design specialist and/or musician visit the students to share expertise in the area of mood. Set up a visual or auditory display showing how sound, colour, or visual patterns can affect or create a mood or atmosphere.

Evaluation

Evaluation should be based on the learning outcomes stated previously. Teachers may wish to include the strategies of observation and student/peer evaluation. See Evaluation section, pp. 95 – 123.

Resources
- A variety of poetry anthologies
- Local educational authority resource materials for:
  Media Literacy
  Dance

3

TEAM PLANNING AND DELIVERY

This model brings together two or more teachers who share their respective subject disciplines to facilitate the investigation of a topic, theme, or issue. This involves collaborative planning, creative timetabling, and team teaching/delivery. This approach is particularly appropriate for developing themes relevant to the four subject clusters identified earlier.

MODEL 1: SUBJECT-BASED
Language

VISUAL ARTS
- express personal feelings and interpret a character or setting in *Harriet's Daughter* through a variety of materials and activities such as modelling, constructing, painting, and drawing

PHYSICAL AND HEALTH EDUCATION
- develop an understanding of the cultural diversity of dance and the ways in which different aspects of society are reflected in dance
- discuss national sports and children's games

GEOGRAPHY
- investigate the Caribbean tourist region
- help students learn about physical features, peoples, and cultures of the Caribbean basin
- understand the positive and negative effects of tourism on Caribbean countries

LANGUAGE

Novel Study: *Harriet's Daughter*
A young Tobagonian girl faces a variety of problems while living in Toronto.
- learn how values are illustrated through folk tales
- learn how folk tales develop out of the social and geographic realities of the people whose culture the tale portrays

HISTORY
- examine changes occurring in society as a result of immigration
- examine the roles of individuals and groups of people in effecting change

MUSIC
- study the musical language and elements related to the genius of music, for example, gospel, reggae, rap
- examine the music of Caribbean societies

FAMILY STUDIES
- examine differences and similarities in parenting roles in various family units
- compare child-rearing practices of the past with those of today
- analyze the historical influence of values, attitudes, and roles on the clothes people choose to wear

DRAMATIC ARTS
- develop story-telling skills
- create tableaux that express events or issues from novel
- develop role-play scenarios

Rationale   Throughout this unit, students will gain an historical perspective on the multicultural mosaic of our society. They will develop an appreciation and respect for the differences and similarities among cultural groups. It is important that students recognize social values and beliefs through concrete experiences.

Learning Outcomes   Learners will:
- demonstrate the ability to articulate their own values
- demonstrate an understanding and appreciation of the contribution of various cultures in society
- acquire knowledge, skills, and values related to the unit through learner-centred teaching
- analyze social, political, environmental and economic issues related to Caribbean communities.

Teacher Planning   This unit could coincide with Black History month held in February. Novels dealing with different cultural backgrounds can also be used in this unit.

   The following suggestions may be helpful:
- Collaboration is required for the success of this unit.
- Approach one or more colleagues, discuss the idea of planning and working together on specific learning outcomes.
- Assess your students' interests and needs with them.
- Schedule meetings in the morning or at lunch time.
- Invite your teacher-librarian and chairpersons/team leaders to your planning meetings.
- Suggest and discuss various ways to deliver and complement the unit, for example:
  - taking advantage of teachers' areas of expertise
  - involving two or more classes in large-group activities
  - asking teachers to host mini-workshops for groups of students moving from one session to another
  - field trips
  - community services
  - community involvement
- For better delivery, schedule blocks of time. Ask your administrative staff for assistance in accomplishing this task.
- After discussion with your colleagues, create a list of possible human resources to invite as guest speakers, for example:
  - local educational authority personnel

- representatives from an appropriate Caribbean consulate(s)
  - dance groups
- Update your students on your planning meetings.
- Discuss and determine assessment with your students and colleagues.
- Try to reach a balance between teacher evaluation and student evaluation.
- Set a date to start the unit.
- Set meeting dates with your colleagues at least once a week during the unit for updates, clarifications, and celebrations.
- After the unit is finished, meet again with your colleagues to assess and evaluate the process and the product.
- Make suggestions for further references.
- Ask your students for their contributions and value their opinions.
- Celebrate your successes.

Sample Activities

Family Studies

1. Invite a local community member to talk about the Caribbean communities.
2. Students could prepare a meal that reflects the tastes of one or more Caribbean communities.
3. Students could provide examples and explanations of the part played by food in their families' religious festivals, traditions, and special events.
4. Have students interview family members and/or examine family photo albums to compare the clothing worn by teenagers today with that worn by their parents and grandparents as teenagers.

Geography

1. Have students design a travel brochure for the Caribbean Islands.
2. On a large classroom map, students could locate and label each of the islands of the Caribbean and the surrounding countries, and draw lines to connect your city/town to each of the islands.
3. Have students write a travel journal of a week's vacation in the Caribbean. Examples of sites, people, and cultural differences could be included.

Music

1. Ask students to bring in or start a steel drum band.

2. Introduce the class to a variety of tapes and compact discs to foster appreciation of different genres of music.
3. Encourage students to write and perform their own reggae or rap composition.

Physical and Health Education

1. Teach students a variety of Caribbean dances.
2. Have students develop a dance segment coordinated with music of their choice.

Visual Arts

1. Students could give their personal interpretation of the main character or setting of *Harriet's Daughter* through a selected artistic medium.
2. Students could show a series of pictures illustrating the variety of settings within *Harriet's Daughter*.

History

1. Ask students to prepare a short biography of Harriet Tubman or map the route of the Underground Railway.
2. Have students prepare a class booklet on the real or imaginary life experiences of early Caribbean settlers based on recorded historical anecdotes.

Language/Drama

1. Students could read or listen to folk tales and discuss the values represented in the literature.
2. Have students compare the effect of reading a folk tale with the effect of hearing it narrated.
3. Ask students to illustrate and dramatize their favourite tale.
4. Ask students to compare and contrast traditions illustrated in folk tales with traditions in their own homes.
5. Ensure that the study of the novel includes examination of characters, setting, theme, plot, and conflict.

Evaluation

For self-evaluation, students could assess a personal piece of work following a set of criteria. For group evaluation, students could evaluate how well the group has worked together. Individual teacher evaluation in the form of tracking/monitoring is possible where progress of individual students is carefully annotated. Collaborative teacher evaluation can occur if teachers meet to discuss and assess a student project or activity.

Resources

- Support documents for each subject area
- sufficient copies of the novel *Harriet's Daughter*
- information from appropriate tourist boards or consulates for print material, and speakers

MODEL 2: INTERDISCIPLINARY
Personal Relationships

PERSONAL RELATIONSHIPS
- with peers
- with family members and other care givers
- with society

GUIDANCE
- examine students' strengths, values, interests, skills, and aptitudes to define self
- work to develop an understanding of others
- learn techniques for dealing with peer pressure

FAMILY STUDIES
- examine the relationship between food habits and family life
- examine ways in which family life changes as circumstances change
- identify current trends in social relationships and how these trends may shape family life in the future

PHYSICAL AND HEALTH EDUCATION
- incorporate cooperative games and skills which promote positive peer relationships
- provide opportunities to discuss issues such as dating, marriage, divorce, and separation
- promote appreciation of similarities and differences in other cultures through the medium of dance

LANGUAGE
- use literature to explore different kinds of relationships
- role-play scenarios to depict various relationships in the student's life
- examine the role of the media in depicting social relationships
- develop positive communication skills

Rationale

The needs of the young adolescent are central to this unit. Peer acceptance, group activities, family interaction, and the perception of self are key components to the integrated theme and related activities. Many opportunities will be afforded to students for designing and shaping the unit.

Learning Outcomes

Learners will:
- demonstrate an understanding of self
- demonstrate respect for the rights, feelings, and dignity of others
- recognize the importance of actively participating in family life, and the life of the school and community
- work cooperatively on common tasks
- resolve conflicts in non-violent ways
- demonstrate appreciation for the rights and responsibilities of all individuals.

Teacher Planning

Blocks of planning time are critical to the success of this unit. Collaborative planning should include:
- meaningful ways to apply curriculum content to the chosen topic
- planning of activities and field trips
- preplanning of large-group activities (such as planning for space in which activities will take place)
- discussion of evaluation strategies.

Since many aspects of the Guidance curriculum are infused throughout all subjects, e.g., relationships with others, affective education, career education, the teacher(s) responsible for Guidance/Student services should facilitate the coordination and delivery of this unit with other staff. This teacher could:
- act as a guest lecturer
- collaboratively deliver a lesson with the subject teacher
- facilitate small-group activities
- provide opportunities for other teachers to team-teach when appropriate

Based on the needs and interests of the young adolescent, students must be given an opportunity to play a significant role in the development and delivery of the integrated unit. Before beginning the unit, involve students in setting the objectives and designing the evaluation criteria. It is extremely important that the balance be struck between teacher-directed and learner-centred activities.

Outside resources to supplement the wide-ranging expertise of the teacher-team might include:

- audio-visual aids
- the media
- professional theatrical groups
- library resources
- curriculum/program resource staff
- community agencies/resources

Most of the unit will take place in individual classrooms, but some activities may require larger areas, so plan accordingly.

The suggested time for this activity is four to five 70-minute periods. The time allotment does not have to be equal for all subjects; for example, novel studies and conflict resolution programs may require a longer period of time.

Sample Activities

Guidance

1. Use or develop a student-interest inventory. This activity could be done in the Language Arts class.
2. Do a mini-unit on group dynamics. For example, while students are in groups, ask them to examine the roles and behaviours of each group member in order to understand what makes a group effective. This activity can be done in collaboration with the Physical Education teacher(s).
3. Provide students with conflict resolution strategies to help deal with peer relationships. This activity can be done in collaboration with the Family Studies teacher(s) or Guidance counsellor(s).

Language

1. Read aloud to the class a novel or several short stories on the theme of peer relationships. Have students compare, contrast, and analyze through discussion the key components of the relationships.
2. Ask the students to highlight the multitude of relationships that exist in their lives through role-play. Students could then share the role-play with other members of the class. Follow-up activities might include response writing, conflict resolution strategies, movie or book reviews, or forecasting future outcomes.
3. Students could gather magazine pictures depicting various kinds of relationships. Using this medium, students could present their findings using creative product presentation, for example, computer simulations, video, music, or drama.
4. Ask students to investigate the role of verbal and non-verbal expression in developing positive communication skills within relationships in different cultural settings.

Note: The issues of body language, "I" statements, and eye contact may be culturally sensitive for some students.

Family Studies

1. Students could visually represent the diverse and changing family units.
2. Have students develop and administer a survey pertaining to a current social issue, e.g., child abuse or spousal assault. Ask them to analyze the results and make recommendations for dealing with the issue.
3. Ask students to look at family relationships and food habits, e.g., time, frequency and location of meals, quantity of food eaten, selection of food, and people with whom food is shared.

Physical Education

1. In small groups, have students develop a cooperative game, teach the game to the rest of the class, and evaluate the success of their efforts. Leadership, responsibility, and respect permeate this activity.
2. Students could go into the community to interview a variety of experts on issues relating to family planning, separation and divorce, violence against women, sexually transmitted diseases, and present their findings to classmates. This activity could be done jointly with the Family Studies teacher(s).
3. Students could be responsible for designing and facilitating a "Be Active" or "Wellness" day to welcome incoming students. This transition activity promotes skills in leadership and mentoring.

Evaluation

In this unit, students could design evaluation criteria for one or more activities. There is the possibility for:
- peer evaluation in which students assess the performance of others based on mutually agreed upon criteria
- teacher evaluation based on the individual student's needs, growth, development, and capabilities
- evaluation based on creativity and appropriateness of product presentation

Resources

- Local educational authority support documents for each subject area
- Outside resources (see Teacher Planning)

MODEL 3: TRANSDISCIPLINARY
Career Exploration

CAREER EXPLORATION
- always begins with self
- looks at personal interests, skills, aptitudes and values
- links personal awareness to educational and career possibilities
- emphasizes impact of change on future decisions and trends

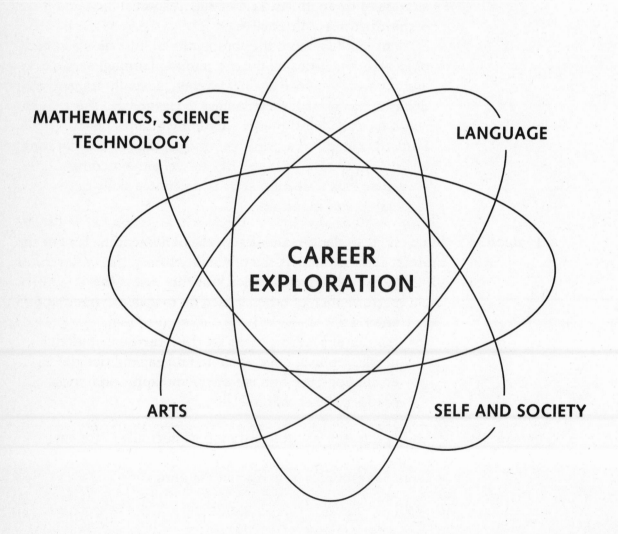

MATHEMATICS, SCIENCE TECHNOLOGY

LANGUAGE

CAREER EXPLORATION

ARTS

SELF AND SOCIETY

Rationale   Career education is an integral part of preparing students for the opportunities, responsibilities, and experiences of adult life. The goal of career education is to increase students' awareness of the choices, changes, and transitions affecting their future. Key components of the program include planned group activities, access to current vocational information, work experience, and life skills.

Learning Outcomes   Learners will:
- acquire information about post-secondary options and opportunities
- acquire a set of transferable skills and behaviours for the future, e.g., teamwork, interpersonal skills, responsibility, and listening skills
- demonstrate an ability to use school and community resources
- demonstrate an understanding of self and the world of work
- demonstrate an ability to make useful decisions.

Teacher Planning

Note: The concept of careers permeates all subjects and day-to-day activities. The relationship between individual subject disciplines and careers (the world of work) must be highlighted whenever appropriate. This will enable students to make meaningful connections between school and the community.

In this sample, the homeroom teacher is responsible for the delivery of Language, Guidance, and Mathematics. Due to the impact of technology on the labour market, this teacher has decided to work with the Design Technology and Science teachers. Activities, out-of-school excursions, and evaluation strategies will be planned collaboratively. It should be noted that:
- blocks of planning time are necessary
- collaborative planning should focus on strategies to emphasize the concept of career exploration in a natural rather than contrived way

Opportunities for team planning might include:
- career fairs
- out-of-school visits
- large-group activities, e.g., two classes together

Based on the needs and interests of the young adolescent, students should be encouraged to discuss and explore the concept of careers. Provide opportunities for extensions and follow-up activities (see Sample Activities, pp. 78 – 80).

Outside resources might include:
- career information software
- audio-visual aids
- Guidance resources
- the media
- library resources
- guest speakers
- job site visits
- visits to colleges and universities
- a career centre
- community agencies

While most activities will take place in the classroom, activities such as Career Days, which require a larger area, must be considered well in advance.

Remember that:
- career education is an ongoing process and should be a part of all curricula
- career exploration, the theme of this unit, is a subtopic which could be effectively dealt with in a four-to-six-week period

Sample Activities

Note: The aim of career education is not to force students to make premature decisions about what they would like to be, but to foster a range of options later in life. How can this be accomplished? First, teachers can provide opportunities for students to understand the connections between self and everything around them (e.g., family, friends, education, leisure, values). It is also important to focus on change and how it influences goals and decisions. This broader definition of career seeks to incorporate both of the above (i.e., self plus change).

It is important to make these connections in a meaningful and natural way. The sample activities have been ordered to show how a teacher might move from an understanding of self to more specific job-related activities.

1. "Values" play an important role in making career decisions. Students should have a clear knowledge of:
   - the term "career education"
   - outside influences that shape one's values, e.g., school, media, family, personal experiences, friends, religion, culture, society

- how and why values can change
- the connection between values and careers

2. In consultation with their teacher-librarian and educational authority or community resource personnel, teachers could gather novels and anthologies that relate to career choices/options. As part of the novel study, students could look for gender patterns, e.g., changing roles, sex role stereotyping, equity (race/colour, sexual orientation, and ability). Through discussion, students could deal with the following issues:
   - the current reality
   - the reasons for changes in current patterns
   - why it is important to play an active role in equity issues

   Note: The aim of this language activity is to show that career education can be subtly infused through literature exploration and other activities done in Language class.

3. a) Select an interest inventory (or develop one yourself) based on the needs of your students. Once completed, allow students to discover how their interests and strengths relate to educational and career planning.

   b) Based on discoveries made above, ask students to select an occupation that interests them. Each student could gather information in order to complete an occupational study.

   Note: The focus is on what the student would like to know about the specific occupation.

   The student is responsible for choosing a method of presenting this information. Invite other teachers/students in to see the presentations. A careers bulletin board could be started in the classroom or in a central area of the school.

4. Ask students to bring in an assortment of want ads. Students could choose one advertisement that appeals to them and complete the following:
   - list reasons for personal appeal, e.g., high salary, work involves animals, independent work, physical activity
   - list personal qualities they bring to the job
   - write a letter applying for this job which includes some information above

5. The name of this activity is "What Is Technology?" Students will acquire a broader understanding of technology by combing their surroundings for examples. Each student is asked to:
   - choose three to five areas such as home, school, shopping mall, or doctor's office

- list as many examples of technology as possible for each area, e.g. in industry, 1. fork lift, 2. _____, 3. _____
- relate findings to educational preparation and job possibilities

6. Ask students to choose an invention and gather the following information:
    - what it is and who invented it
    - description of its early stages
    - description of changes that have occurred to improve the product
    - predictions for the future of this invention, i.e., obsolescence or continued improvements
    - purposes that the invention serves
    - skills necessary to be an inventor

Note: Steven Caney's *Invention Book* is a great resource for this activity.

7. a) Incorporate a unit on banking in your core program. Organize a visit to a bank or trust company in your community. Ask students to develop an interview outline for conducting an interview with managers, loan officers, tellers, and other staff.
    Follow-up discussions or extension activities might deal with jobs available in banking, future trends in banking, budgeting, or finances.
    b) Use current career information such as employment figures, salary ranges, and gender breakdowns when dealing with skills such as graphing, ratio and percent, and problem-solving.

8. Technology consists of broad-based areas: communication, construction, design, manufacturing, services, and transportation. Divide the class into six groups. Each group is responsible for one area of technology. Through discussion and/or research, the group will look at how people did things 100 years ago, how they do them today, and how they will do them differently 100 years from now. Findings will be shared with the rest of the class.

Evaluation The teachers involved in this particular sample could collaborate to develop an independent study project such as "Careers in the Community," "Technological Changes in Our World," or "School and Careers." Parts of the finished project could be evaluated collaboratively, while other parts could be evaluated on an individual basis (see Evaluation section, pp. 95 – 123).

Teachers could also develop a quiz/test dealing with general career concept ideas (i.e., Have the students grasped the importance of the connection(s) between school and career paths?)

Teachers should remember to use a variety of assessment/evaluation strategies throughout the course of this unit.

Resources

- Local educational authority Guidance documents

- School or public library

- Government career centres

- Community colleges and universities

- Guest speakers

- Novels that support career exploration, such as:
  Linda Crew, *Children of the River*. Dell, 1991.
  Joyce Hansen, *The Gift-Giver*. Houghton-Mifflin, 1980.
  Joy Kogawa, *Naomi's Road*. Oxford, 1988.
  Jean Little, *From Anna*. Harper Collins, 1972.

The following titles would also be useful if available in the library resource centre:
Geoffrey Bilson, *Death over Montreal*.
Janne Carlsson, *Camel Bells*.
Marsha Hewitt, et. al., *One Proud Summer*.
Elizabeth Laird, *Kiss the Dust*.
Barbara Smucker, *Days of Terror*.

MODEL 3: TRANSDISCIPLINARY
Utopian Country
(School-wide theme)

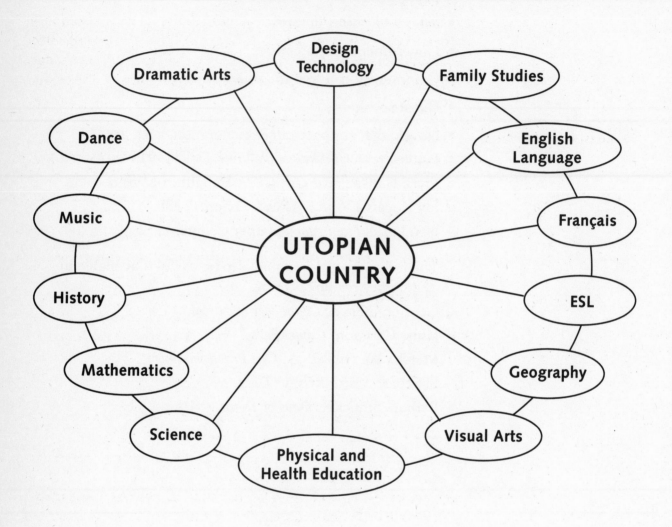

Rationale   The focus of a school-wide theme is to encourage students, teachers, parents, and administrators to work on a common goal within a contextual framework. This model addresses several needs of the young adolescent, e.g., the need to engage in connected and relevant learning, to incorporate a variety of teaching and learning styles, and to develop positive interpersonal skills.

Throughout this unit students will explore, read, and apply their knowledge and communication skills to create a utopian country through an integrated approach. They will carry out their assignment with the support and guidance of the entire school staff.

Learning Outcomes   Learners will:
- access, retrieve, utilize, and evaluate information using a variety of technologies
- read and analyze information from a variety of sources
- use their knowledge in the arts, mathematics, science, technology, and social science to write paragraphs
- apply communication skills in all areas of the curriculum
- observe form, shape, patterns, movement, and inter-relationships in nature
- apply scientific, geographic, political, social, ecological, and economic knowledge to analyze current global issues and trends
- demonstrate a respect for the rights, feelings, and dignity of other human beings
- use critical and creative thinking models to formulate and solve problems and make decisions
- demonstrate an understanding of the role of technology in the home, school, and community
- gain access to and use reliable, relevant sources of information to deal with problems or issues.

Teacher Planning   This sample unit is based on a school-wide theme developed at a middle school. It lasted five weeks and closed with an Open House to celebrate the students' achievement.

The needs of the young adolescent must be the main focus of the theme; in other words, students should be given ownership of the project. Before commencing, teachers, teachers' aides, and administrators should discuss the benefits and implications of such an integrated unit.

The following elements should be considered:
- school climate
- issues involved in working together
- many facets of the curriculum delivered through the unit
- changes in school life for this period, e.g., higher student traffic in the hallways

Collaborative staff planning is the key element to the success of this unit. There are different ways to start. Large blocks of time are necessary in the preliminary planning stages. At least two half-days will be required.

Identify teachers interested in planning the unit and designate a chairperson. It is important to encourage representation from all subject areas.

At the first meeting:
- present the task of looking for a school-wide theme
- set the parameters, i.e., ensure the theme is directly related to the needs of the young adolescent learner, parents and staff, educational authority policies, and school goals
- brainstorm ideas and accept all suggestions
- choose the theme

Next, discuss the following:
- learning outcomes
- knowledge, skills, values, and attitudes
- time frame
- assessment and evaluation
- changes in routines and scheduling
- resources available to develop activities and to provide support for teachers
- closure for theme, e.g., festival, open house
- flow of student traffic in the school

At the second meeting, on a flip chart:
- list all subject disciplines
- list the compulsory elements of the unit
- list all ideas and activities related to the theme (see pp. 86 – 90)

Note: In this particular school, the charts were displayed in the teacher resource area.

- discuss various assessment and evaluation strategies — be prepared to present different techniques to the staff who may feel apprehensive about holistic assessment
- work with your teacher-librarian to gather pertinent resources

- plan short after-school or lunch-time meetings to address staff concerns
- encourage staff to be flexible with classroom time, e.g., students may need time in Geography to complete an Art assignment
- consider developing a guest speaker list, a list of community services, and site visits
- discuss how to represent this activity on the report card

The school spent approximately five weeks on this unit, representing approximately one third of the term; one third of the final mark came from this unit.

Further Considerations for the Planning Committee:

With your administration:
- encourage them to be involved — students need to feel that the entire school staff is working collaboratively
- keep your principal up-to-date on the development of the theme
- discuss concerns of teachers, students, or parents
- with your principal, inform parents/guardians of the school-wide theme in a letter that covers:
  - rationale
  - description of theme
  - student expectations
  - learning outcomes
  - assignments and deadlines
  - assessment and evaluation strategies
  - first language/bilingual provisions for equity of outcome
- involve International language staff — by acting as translators, they can help parents understand the full meaning of the integrated unit

With the custodial staff:
- discuss any changes in routine which may affect their duties

With the teaching staff:
- plan a closing activity for the theme, e.g., festival of countries, open house, parents' night
- set the location, time, and date, and prepare invitations
- set a date for a staff meeting following your closing activity for feedback, general comments, and suggestions

In the classroom, homeroom teachers should set aside four 40-minute periods to discuss the following:
- the main elements of the theme

- compulsory elements to be included
- expectations with respect to behaviour, assignments, deadlines
- assessment and evaluation strategies to be used
- student groupings

Teachers now take their classes to look at the chart listing the ideas/activities. Collaboratively, students and teachers choose the components of their unit from the list. Teachers can choose two or three ideas/activities.

Students then fill out goal sheets based on each subject, listing the area they will research. Special supplies that will be needed should be ordered, and presentation requirements (special materials, AV equipment) should be submitted to teachers for booking. Decisions regarding the presentation format and date of presentation need to be made early in the unit.

Invite other teachers and classes for your students' presentations. Presentations:
- can take place in the homeroom classroom
- should be delivered as an integrated final product including all of the student's research from all subject areas. The French component of the unit, for example, can be delivered in French during the presentation.

The week of presentations should be celebration week. Invite parents, trustees, administrators, colleagues from other schools, support staff.

Suggested time: This particular unit required five weeks utilizing 75% of each day.

Below can be found the content of the charts that were placed in a common area for teacher and student consultation in preparation for their utopian country.

Compulsory Elements for the Unit

Discuss the following with the students before undertaking any research. Stress that these concepts constitute the structure of the unit.

Location of the utopian country
- climate
- flora/fauna
- travel
- trade and industries
- food and clothing
- natural resources
- landscape

Political system of the utopian country
- type
- military
- constitution
- languages
- immigration
- emigration

History of the utopian country
- changes, evolution
- revolution
- founding societies and peoples
- explorers
- territories/colonies

Culture of the utopian country
- architecture
- music
- literature
- sports
- languages
- fine arts
- cuisine
- folk arts, crafts
- religion
- values
- morals
- family structures
- multiculturalism

Science and technology of the utopian country
- plants
- medical research
- communications/telecommunications
- transportation
- research and development
- business
- space program
- computer technology

Economy of the utopian country
- products
- manufactures
- profitability
- money systems
- math systems

- investments
- taxes
- trade, free trade
- stock exchange
- foundations of the economy

A second chart should be posted as follows:
Ideas/Activities Related to the Utopian Country by Subject Discipline

Art
- travel brochure
- mapping
- illustrations of myths and legends
- coat of arms
- statues of important people
- design of a city square
- new flag
- masks, costumes, fashion design
- mascot for sports' team
- model of artifacts
- design of room for National Gallery
- jewelry
- historical plaques
- archaeological finds
- architecture

English
- relevant poems and articles on utopia
- media study
- variety of relevant literary genres
- history of the flag
- reading out loud from one of the country's masterpieces

Dance
- festivals, carnivals, rituals
- origin of dance in the country
- national dance(s)
- importance of dance in the country's culture

Design Technology
- urban planning
- types of communications
- non polluting vehicles

Drama
- role-play

English as a Second Language
- all or part of the presentation could be done in the student's first language (assistance from translators may be needed)

Family Studies	• national dress
	• national dish
	• family units
Français	• légendes, mythes
	• héros/héroines
	• histoire du pays
	• charte des droits de la personne
	• hymne national en français
	• motto
	• drapeau et son histoire
	• vocabulaire specifique à ce pays
	• temps des verbes à utiliser
	• genres littéraires
	• média
Geography	• mapping
	• climatograph
	• physical patterns
	• river systems
	• land-locked features
	• natural resources
	• industries
	• imports/exports
	• transportation
	• tourism
	• cultures
History	• explorers
	• legends, myths
	• government
	• revolution or change
	• voting system
	• lineage/genealogy
	• flag, coat of arms, motto, languages
	• border countries
	• minorities
	• equity among the peoples
	• multicultural society
	• basics of negotiation
	• charter of rights
	• judicial system
	• legal implications
	• constitution
	• rituals, festivals

Mathematics	• currency
	• trade
	• census
	• scale
	• graphing
	• mapping
	• statistics
	• referendum predictions
Music	• national anthem
	• famous composers
Physical and Health Education	• national sport
	• create your own sport or game
	• uniforms
	• professional teams
	• funding for Olympic teams
Science	• environment problems
	• diseases
	• flora and fauna
	• energy forms and crises
	• industries and machinery
	• communication systems
	• animals
	• ecosystem

Evaluation

The integrated nature of this unit calls for ongoing assessment and evaluation. Strategies must be discussed and accepted by all teachers before beginning the unit. Process is equally important in the evaluation. The final product is evaluated by the homeroom teachers in consultation with other teachers. Each subject teacher uses a variety of evaluation instruments after teaching certain skills. Those marks are used when determining the final mark.

Resources

The planning committee should establish a list of resources available. These will include educational authority guidelines and support documents, school/local library resources, local professional library, community agencies, guest speakers, museums, families, students, and other staff members.

ASSESSMENT
AND
EVALUATION

Assessment and Evaluation: The Big Picture

Assessment and evaluation are part of an ongoing daily process which examines the whole person in the school setting. This process enables every student regardless of culture, learning exceptionality, or language facility to have the opportunity for success in school and in life.

Because evaluation is not an end in itself, but a part of the learning process for both the student and the teacher, assessment and evaluation must be student-centred. This helps to ensure that students become problem solvers, decision makers, effective communicators, and independent learners.

It is important to highlight the difference between assessment and evaluation:

Assessment   The gathering and recording of data about a student. This process is ongoing and occurs daily. As a result, opportunities for individual program modification will occur.

Evaluation   The interpretation of the data collected in order to measure student achievement and growth.

Only when evaluation is a part of the teacher's overall planning, and is related to learning outcomes and choice of teaching strategies, can the needs of the young adolescent (i.e., varied ability levels, a need to see connections, the importance of peer relationships) be met.

Effective evaluation must:

- be planned by the teacher and incorporate student contributions
- establish a balance between process and product
- employ a variety of approaches and techniques including self and peer evaluation
- foster the student's self-esteem
- be unbiased
- be clearly understood by students, parents, guardians, and administration
- meet the needs of exceptional and ESL students
- provide opportunities for individual program modification, e.g., student remediation/enrichment
- provide opportunities for students to apply knowledge, skills, and values in authentic situations — ones that reflect or simulate the world beyond the classroom.

When selecting assessment and evaluation strategies appropriate to the classroom program, it is important to address the student first. There is a strong connection between the characteristics and needs of the young adolescent and each strategy suggested below. However, these characteristics and needs could be addressed using various other strategies — there is, in fact, a wide range of strategies employed in the evaluation process.

CHARACTERISTICS AND NEEDS OF THE YOUNG ADOLESCENT	STRATEGY	INSTRUMENTS
• concerns are immediate	• observation	• daily work • participation in group activities • student behaviours • tracking and monitoring • anecdotal records • checklists
• relationship with a significant, caring adult • affirmation	• conference	• with other students • with teachers • with parent(s)/guardian(s)
• variations in ability/ performance level	• work samples done individually and in small groups	• assignments • oral presentations • projects • portfolios
• leadership and responsibility • validation of self • peer and social acceptance	• self, peer, and group evaluation	• diaries, logs • pieces of work • discussion
• structure – time management and study skills	• tests and exams	• homework assignments • quizzes • formal examinations • standardized and diagnostic tests
• research, problem-solving and decision-making • setting and assessing goals	• independent study	• research projects • debates • mock trials • student surveys and inventories

SAMPLE INSTRUMENTS FOR ASSESSMENT AND EVALUATION

In each of the sections that follow, one aspect of evaluation is addressed and tips are provided to help teachers. Sample instruments have been included to assist teachers as they consider each of the specific techniques.

In some cases, the instrument has been filled in to show how the process could be undertaken. As well, a blank copy has been provided for teacher use.

EVALUATION

Make sure comments are based on behaviour and are **measurable** insofar as possible. While observation is an ongoing process, it does not have to be done every day for every student.

- Choose two to three students to monitor each day.
- Information collected must be well-organized for later reference. Find a system that suits you (e.g., portfolio, computer spreadsheet).
- When observing student behaviour, look for **patterns** of behaviour, not behaviour in isolation.

Anecdotal Comment Sheet

NAME: _____

SUBJECT AREA	SEPTEMBER	OCTOBER	NOVEMBER
Personal Development • leadership • group interactions • organization • independence and initiative • effort/attitude	• cooperative • contributes ideas • consistently meets deadlines • accepts and learns from constructive criticism		
Language	• additional work on revision and editing process needed • personal writing is thoughtful and open		

History	• grasps central issues
	• project work
	  • well organized
	  • creative final product		

Geography	• good mapping skills
	• class work:
	  • on task
	  • homework sometimes incomplete		

Mathematics	• needs additional review in Integers and Tessellations • concrete examples helpful		
	Note: Subject headings will change for individual teachers. Anecdotal notation should be specific but can include a wide variety of information, i.e., product results, home contacts, behaviours, skill development.		

Anecdotal Comment Sheet

NAME: _____

SUBJECT AREA	SEPTEMBER	OCTOBER	NOVEMBER

Tracking and Monitoring Checklist

NAME: _____

Subject/Topic/ Activity	Contributes ideas	Works independently	Listens to others	Exhibits commitment	Meets Deadlines	Shows understanding		
History: Rebellions Class Discussion *Date: November 13*	✓ often	✓ self-motivated	Tends to interrupt	✓	N.A.	✓ good		
Math: Fractions Taking up homework *Date: November 26*	✓ often	N.A.	Interrupts frequently	✓	Homework always done on time	✓ excellent		
Date:								
Mode: to be determined by teacher – mark, check, or comment.								

Note: The headings will change depending on the teacher's classroom program and reporting needs.

Tracking and Monitoring Checklist

NAME: _____

Subject/Topic/Activity								
Date:								
Date:								
Date:								

In this instance, the project is shaped, developed, and delivered by the student in consultation with the teacher. This strategy should be used to help students acquire and develop the following skills and attitudes: self-motivation, time management (deadlines), organization, and general thinking.

- Regular conferences with students enable teachers to assist in and monitor the process.
- Encourage risk-taking, problem-solving and decision-making.
- This technique can be used individually or with groups of students.
- Teacher assistance might be provided in the following areas: setting deadlines, establishing goals, and using resources both inside and outside the classroom.

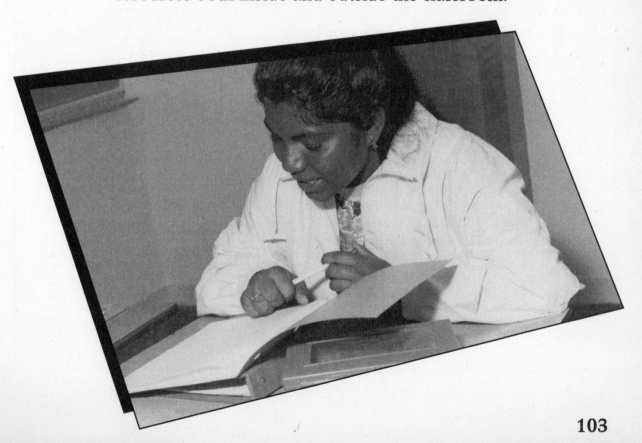

Independent Study Proposal

NAME(S): _____

PROJECT ASSIGNED ON: _February 1_

The topic I have chosen is: _Organizing a rock concert_

_____

My intended audience is: _My classmates_

What I already know about the topic is: _Contemporary rock groups,_ _sound systems, etc._

Possible resources for more information might be: _Going to a music_ _studio interviewing agents, fundraisers._

I will present my final product in the following manner: _Video, pictures,_ _audio tapes, and a written summation._

Important dates: Student/teacher conferences: _Feb 8 (proposal) Feb 22_

March 3

Submission of draft copy: _March 10_

Presentation of final product: _March 17_

Note: This sample may be used (by students) for individual or group projects.

Independent Study Proposal

NAME(S): _____

PROJECT ASSIGNED: _____

The topic I have chosen is: _____
_____
_____

My intended audience is: _____
_____

What I already know about the topic is: _____
_____
_____
_____
_____

Possible resources for more information might be: _____
_____
_____

I will present my final product in the following manner: _____
_____
_____

Important dates: Student/teacher conferences: _____
                                          _____

                Submission of draft copy: _____

                Presentation of final product: _____

Teacher Evaluation

NAME: _____

PROJECT TITLE: ___ROCK CONCERT_____

ORIGINALITY/CREATIVITY

- Wide range of presentation forms.
- Pieced together creatively.

`/20`

ORGANIZATION/CLARITY

- Good flow of ideas.
- Spoke too quickly in oral presentation.
- Written submission lacked accuracy.

`/25`

RESEARCH SKILLS

- primary _Interviewed agents, lighting technicians, musicians, managers of concert hall, and peers._
- secondary _Researched music magazines, library resources, watched videos._

`/25`

OVERALL IMPRESSION

- Effort was evident.
- Good audience participation.
- Audio-visual kept interest high.
- Occasionally lost focus.

`/10`

SELF-EVALUATION

In general, I feel that my final presentation was _awesome. I enjoyed doing it because I am really interested in rock music. My friends told me they really enjoyed it._

`/20`

FINAL EVALUATION

Teacher: _____

Student: _____

Total: [   ]

Signature(s): ___Teacher A/B___

Teacher Evaluation

NAME: _____

PROJECT TITLE: _____

ORIGINALITY/CREATIVITY

_____

_____

_____

_____

_____ ☐

ORGANIZATION/CLARITY

_____

_____

_____

_____

_____ ☐

RESEARCH SKILLS

• primary _____

_____

_____

• secondary _____

_____

_____ ☐

OVERALL IMPRESSION

_____

_____

_____

_____

_____ ☐

SELF-EVALUATION

In general, I feel that my final presentation

was _____

_____

_____

_____ ☐

FINAL EVALUATION

Teacher: _____

Student: _____

Total: ☐

Signature(s): _____

EVALUATION

CONFERENCE TIPS

A conference should be well-planned and student expectations should be made clear. Frequency of conferences depends upon the needs of the individual students.

Teacher feedback should be immediate and practical. Openness, acceptance, and constructive criticism are key elements.

Conference Record Sheet

STUDENT: _____ DATE: _____

Assignment or topic discussed: _____
_____

Student comment: _____
_____
_____

Teacher comment: _____
_____
_____

Next step: _____
_____
_____

- -

Conference Record Sheet

STUDENT: _____ DATE: _____

Assignment or topic discussed: _____
_____

Student comment: _____
_____
_____

Teacher comment: _____
_____
_____

Next step: _____
_____
_____

EVALUATION

SELF, PEER, GROUP TIPS

It is important for students to understand the **value** of assessing personal performance. Use this strategy where appropriate and when the evaluation criteria have been clearly explained.

An atmosphere of trust and honesty must exist before proceeding.

Teachers must accept and give value to student contributions regarding assessment and evaluation.

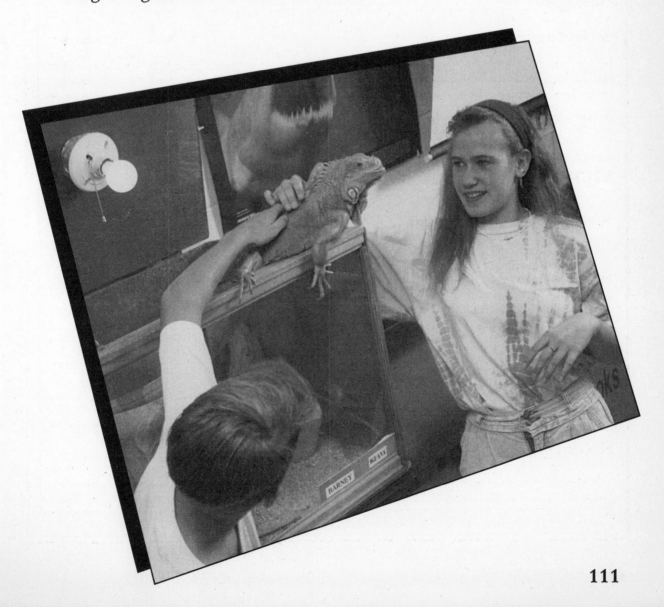

Self-Evaluation Sheet

NAME: _____

DATE: _____

Choose the most accurate letter for each statement.

O = Often
R = Rarely

	Student	Teacher
1. I help other members of my group.	☐	☐
2. I share my ideas with my group.	☐	☐
3. I let others help me.	☐	☐
4. I help other members understand the work.	☐	☐
5. I praise members in my group.	☐	☐
6. I try to stay on task.	☐	☐
7.	☐	☐
8.	☐	☐

Two areas that I need to improve: _____

_____

_____

_____

_____

_____

Self-Evaluation Sheet

NAME: _____

DATE: _____

Weekly/Monthly/Term Review

1. Completion of my assignments:

    _____ All my assignments were handed in by the due date.

    _____ Most of my assignments were handed in by the due date.

    However, _____ assignment(s) were late.

2. My viewpoint on the quality of the work I completed is:

    _____ High quality work

    _____ Good work

    _____ Fair work

    _____ I need to improve in some areas, specifically _____

3. My work in groups was:

    ☆☆☆☆☆ _____ ☆☆☆☆ _____ ☆☆☆ _____ ☆☆ _____ ☆ _____

4. My overall behaviour was:

    ☆☆☆☆☆ _____ ☆☆☆☆ _____ ☆☆☆ _____ ☆☆ _____ ☆ _____

5. This week/month/term I was pleased with: _____

    _____

    _____

    Next week/month/term I will work harder at: _____

    _____

    _____

    The most interesting thing I learned was: _____

    _____

    _____

LOOKING BACK...
At my assignment/test/week/presentation

NAME: _____

DATE: _____

Some things I/we did: _____
_____
_____
_____
_____

The things I learned well enough to teach someone else are: _____
_____
_____
_____
_____

Something I am unsure about/disappointed with: _____
_____
_____
_____
_____

The best part of my/our work was: _____
_____
_____
_____
_____

Peer Evaluation: Oral Presentation

STUDENT'S NAME: _____

EVALUATOR'S NAME: _____

	VG	G	NI

Body Language
- Presenter was confident
- Presenter established eye contact with audience

Voice and Projection
- Presenter spoke with a pleasant, clear voice

Introduction
- Captured the audience's interest

Ending
- Strong and memorable
- Summed up the presentation

Organization
- Used interesting visuals
- Involved the audience
- Used notes/cue cards
- Invited and answered questions from the audience
- Kept within time frame

VG = Very Good
G = Good
NI = Needs
    Improvement

Evaluation of Another Group's Presentation

GROUP: _____

DATE: _____

1. List three things you learned in the presentation.

2. How did the group demonstrate creativity?

3. What change(s) would you suggest to the group for improvement?

4. What else would you like to learn about the topic?

EVALUATION
REPORTING TO PARENTS

In view of the new focus on the needs of the young adolescent, and the emphasis on holistic assessment and evaluation, many schools are moving toward a balance between anecdotal and traditional reporting procedures. The information collected through observation, conferences, student assessment, and other means forms the basis for this approach to reporting. An examination of all facets of the learner's experience will better define stages of development, progress, and performance.

Included in this section are representative samples of student progress reports from two school boards.

NAME OF LOCAL EDUCATIONAL AUTHORITY

Learner ....

Placement .... Room No. ....

Homeroom Teacher ....

School ....

Date ....

Teacher Observations/Recommendations:

Days Absent to Date .... Times Late to Date ....

Teacher .... Principal ....

Placement in September 19___

INDIVIDUAL GROWTH AND DEVELOPMENT

Frequently Observed
Sometimes Observed
Rarely Observed

This has been completed in relation to behaviour observed in the learner's homeroom and other classes.

PERSONAL DEVELOPMENT
Shows self-confidence....................
Has enthusiasm for learning................
Shows initiative........................
Learns from his or her mistakes............
Accepts responsibility for own behaviour......

SOCIAL DEVELOPMENT
Respects rights and opinions of others......
Participates in group activities..........
Co-operates with peers and teachers........
Uses problem-solving skills in social situations...

LEARNING SKILLS
Knows how to gather information............
Displays organizational abilities..........
Makes useful interpretations from the information....
Asks meaningful questions..................
Makes logical predictions..................
Uses problem solving strategies............
Communicates ideas effectively............
Concentrates on and completes tasks........
Applies learning in new situations..........

TO LEARNERS AND PARENTS
You are encouraged to keep this record for future reference. A copy has been placed in the learner's school record folder.

KEY: E - Experiencing difficulty   B - Beginning to progress
A - Appropriate progress   O - Outstanding progress

LANGUAGE

LANGUAGE ARTS

ORAL LANGUAGE

Achievement
Low ☐☐☐☐☐ High

	E	B	A	O
Listens to gather information.				
Expresses ideas clearly.				
Participates co-operatively in small group talks.				

WRITING

Writes for many purposes.				
Expresses ideas clearly.				
Revises and edits accurately.				

READING

Stage of Reading Development _____

Shows an understanding of content.				
Explores and retells ideas in print and other media.				
Responds to personally chosen materials.				
Reads independently for enjoyment.				

FRENCH

Achievement
Low ☐☐☐☐☐ High

	E	B	A	O
Participates with interest and enthusiasm.				
Listens and speaks with understanding.				
Has good pronunciation.				
Reads with understanding.				

MATHEMATICS, SCIENCE AND TECHNOLOGY

Learner: ....

MATHEMATICS

Achievement
Low ☐☐☐☐☐ High

	E	B	A	O
Understands number and operations.				
Understands concepts and procedures.				
Uses estimation strategies.				
Expresses mathematical ideas clearly.				
Applies knowledge to solve problems.				

SCIENCE

Achievement
Low ☐☐☐☐☐ High

	E	B	A	O
Poses and solves problems.				
Makes and records accurate measurements.				
Understands applications and implications of science.				

DESIGN AND TECHNOLOGY

Achievement
Low ☐☐☐☐☐ High

	E	B	A	O
Participates with interest and enthusiasm.				
Understands and applies skills.				
Uses a variety of materials and tools appropriately.				
Uses problem solving strategies in design.				

ARTS KEY: E - Experiencing difficulty B - Beginning to progress
A - Appropriate progress O - Outstanding progress

VISUAL ARTS

Achievement
Low ☐☐☐☐☐ High

	E	B	A	O
Communicates ideas and feelings through art.				
Uses a variety of materials and tools appropriately.				
Demonstrates creativity.				

MUSIC

Achievement
Low ☐☐☐☐☐ High

	E	B	A	O
Participates with interest and enthusiasm.				
Explores ideas and feelings through music.				
Understands rhythm, pitch, harmony, form and dynamics.				

This section may not be assessed for every student.

INSTRUMENTAL MUSIC

Achievement
Low ☐☐☐☐☐ High

	B	A	O
Performs with skill.			
Participates with interest and enthusiasm.			
Cares for instrument.			

DRAMATIC ARTS

Achievement
Low ☐☐☐☐☐ High

	B	A	O
Participates with interest and enthusiasm.			
Explores ideas and feelings through drama.			

SELF AND SOCIETY Learner: ....

GEOGRAPHY

Achievement
Low ☐☐☐☐☐ High

	E	B	A	O
Understands and applies knowledge of concepts.				
Understands and uses geographic skills.				
Understands the interaction between people and the environment.				

HISTORY

Achievement
Low ☐☐☐☐☐ High

	E	B	A	O
Participates with interest and enthusiasm.				
Communicates ideas and opinions effectively.				
Applies ideas and knowledge to both past and/or present situations.				

FAMILY STUDIES

Achievement
Low ☐☐☐☐☐ High

	E	B	A	O
Participates with interest and enthusiasm.				
Demonstrates skills important to a home.				
Uses a variety of materials and tools appropriately.				

PHYSICAL & HEALTH EDUCATION

Achievement
Low ☐☐☐☐☐ High

	E	B	A	O
Participates with interest and enthusiasm.				
Demonstrates skills necessary for a healthy life-style.				
Demonstrates skills development.				

PROGRESS REPORT - MIDDLE LEVEL
Page 1 of 3

Student _____

Class _____ Date _____

Staff Adviser _____

Days absent this term _____ Times late this term _____

EVALUATION KEY:
N - needs improvement S - satisfactory VG - very good O - outstanding
Items not checked do not apply to this level or to this term.
M - indicates modified program for exceptional student.

Local School Name and Address

Support Services	Level of Service	Teacher
English as a Second Language	_____	_____
English Skills Development	_____	_____
Special Education	_____	_____
Other Services	_____	_____

Mathematics

<50 50-59 60-69 70-79 80-89 90+
☐ ☐ ☐ ☐ ☐ ☐

	N	S	VG	O
• concepts				
• skills				
• application				

Teacher _____

Language Arts / English

<50 50-59 60-69 70-79 80-89 90+
☐ ☐ ☐ ☐ ☐ ☐

	N	S	VG	O
• concepts				
• skills				
• attitudes				

Teacher _____

Social Studies Geography / History

<50 50-59 60-69 70-79 80-89 90+
☐ ☐ ☐ ☐ ☐ ☐

	N	S	VG	O
• concepts				
• skills				
• attitudes				

Teacher _____

Student _____

Class _____ Date _____

EVALUATION KEY:
N - needs improvement   **S** - satisfactory   **VG** - very good   **O** - outstanding
Items not checked do not apply to this level or to this term.
M - indicates modified program for exceptional student.

Local School Name and Address

French

	<50	50-59	60-69	70-79	80-89	90+
N						
S						
VG						
O						

- understanding
- speaking
- reading
- writing

_____ Teacher

Music

	<50	50-59	60-69	70-79	80-89	90+
N						
S						
VG						
O						

- participation
- skills
- appreciation

_____ Teacher

Physical and Health Education

	<50	50-59	60-69	70-79	80-89	90+
N						
S						
VG						
O						

- group interaction
- skills
- health concepts

_____ Teacher

Visual Arts

	<50	50-59	60-69	70-79	80-89	90+
N						
S						
VG						
O						

- concepts
- skills
- appreciation

_____ Teacher

Design and Technology

	<50	50-59	60-69	70-79	80-89	90+
N						
S						
VG						
O						

- concepts
- skills
- attitudes

_____ Teacher

Dramatic Arts

	<50	50-59	60-69	70-79	80-89	90+
N						
S						
VG						
O						

- participation
- skills
- appreciation

_____ Teacher

Family Studies

	<50	50-59	60-69	70-79	80-89	90+
N						
S						
VG						
O						

- concepts
- skills
- attitudes

_____ Teacher

Science

	<50	50-59	60-69	70-79	80-89	90+
N						
S						
VG						
O						

- concepts
- skills
- application

_____ Teacher

PROGRESS REPORT - MIDDLE LEVEL
Page 3 of 3

Local School Name and Address

Student _____ Date _____

Class _____

Student Observations

Co-curricular Activities

_____

_____

Self-Evaluation

_____

_____

_____

Goals for Next Term

_____

_____

_____

_____
Student

Personal Growth and Development

EVALUATION KEY:
N - needs improvement   **S** - satisfactory

Student	Staff Adviser	
		cooperates with others
		respects the rights and feelings of others
		takes pride in the environment
		makes decisions thoughtfully
		accepts responsibility
		shows positive attitude
		takes pride in quality of work
		helps others
		shows commitment to learning

Staff Adviser Observations/Recommendations

_____
Staff Adviser

September placement   _____
                             Principal / Vice Principal

Copies of this report are to be distributed: #1 to parents.; #2 in OSR; #3 to staff adviser

123

GLOSSARY

Note: The following terms are defined according to the way they are used in this document.

Assessment	The gathering and recording of data about a student.
Authentic Assessment	Assessment of student performance on tasks of significance involving the criteria used by experts in the field.
Benchmarks	The standards by which something can be measured or judged based on a predetermined set of criteria.
Collaboration	Cooperation with others in the planning, development, delivery, and assessment of program.
Cross-Curricular Learning Outcomes	Learnings essential to all subject areas.
Core Program	A number of subjects delivered to a group of students by one or more teachers.
Curriculum Integration	The bringing together of the knowledge, skills, and perspectives of different subject areas to aid the exploration of a topic, theme, or issue of relevance to the learner.
Early Adolescence	The ages from 10 to 14 — a particularly challenging period because transitions are occurring in every area: physical, social, emotional, and intellectual.
Evaluation	The interpretation of the data collected in order to measure student achievement and growth.
Interdisciplinary	The involvement of several subjects in partnership as part of an investigation which crosses subject boundaries.
Interest Inventory	An instrument used to measure student interest/skills/attitudes.
Mixed-Ability Grouping	The heterogeneous groupings of students.

ö038

Negotiated Classroom	Students' knowledge, interests, and inclinations are taken into account in all aspects of the program, including planning, use of time, space, topics, activities, and evaluation.
Outcome-Based Classroom	The organization of all programs and instructional efforts around clearly defined learning outcomes students should demonstrate when they leave school.
School Climate/Culture	A shared set of norms, values, and beliefs which enhance or impede student achievement.
Learner-Centred Teaching	A philosophy of education that results in the use of strategies based on the identified needs of learners, both as individuals and as members of an age group.
Student Outcomes	Demonstrations of what students know, can do, and are like.
Subject-Based Integration	The involvement of one subject area as a primary component in a unit along with the skills, insights, and content of other subjects to extend the study.
Theme	A broad issue or idea which goes beyond the boundaries of subject areas.
Topic	A subject-based approach that is usually concrete and sharply defined.
Transdisciplinary	The investigation of a theme focusing on a common essential learning or concept rather than a traditional body of knowledge.
Transition Years	Grades 7–10, in which the curriculum emphasizes the needs of young adolescents, ages 10 to 14.

SUGGESTED READINGS

Beane, J.A. (1990). *A Middle School Curriculum: From Rhethoric to Reality*. Columbus, OH: National Middle School Association.

Egan, K. (1992). *Imagination in Teaching and Learning*. London, ON: Althouse Press.

Fogarty, R. (1991). *The Mindful School: How to Integrate the Curricula*, Palatine, IL: IRI/Skylight Publishing.

Fullan, M.G. and Hargreaves, A. (1991). *What's Worth Fighting For? Working Together for Your School*. Toronto, ON: The Ontario Public School Teachers Federation.

Gamberg, R. (1988). *Learning and Loving It: Theme Studies in the Classroom*. Toronto, ON: OISE Press.

George, P.S. Et al (1992). *The Middle School — And Beyond*. Alexandria, VA: Association for Supervision and Curriculum Development.

Hargreaves, A. and Earl, L. (1991). *Rights of Passage: A Review of Selected Research About Schooling in the Transition Years*, Toronto, ON: OISE Press.

Hart-Hewins, L., Goldman, N., and Parkin, F. (1993). *Integrated Programs for Adolescents*. Markham, ON: Pembroke Publishers.

Hart-Hewins, L. and Wells, J. (1992). *Read It in the Classroom*. Markham, ON: Pembroke Publishers.

Jacobs, H.H. (1989). *Interdisciplinary Curriculum: Design and Implementation*. Alexandria, VA: Association for Supervision and Curriculum Development.

Miller, J.P. (1990). *Holistic Learning: A Teacher's Guide to Integrated Studies*. Toronto, ON: OISE Press.

Oppenheimer, J. (1990). *Getting It Right: Meeting the Needs of the Early Adolescent Learner*. Toronto, ON: Federation of Women Teachers' Associations of Ontario.

Parkin, F. and Sidnell, F. (1994). *E.S.L. Is Everybody's Business*. Markham, ON: Pembroke Publishers.

Educational Leadership, 49(3) (1991). Integrating the Curriculum.

The Intermediate Program: Learning in British Columbia Response Draft (1990). Victoria, BC: British Columbia Ministry of Education.

Orbit, 23(2) (1992). Holistic Education in Practice.

SUGGESTED THEMES FOR CURRICULUM INTEGRATION

ADAPTATION

AESTHETICS

BELIEFS

CAREER EXPLORATION

CARING

CHANGE

CITIZENSHIP

COMMUNICATION

COMMUNITIES

CONFLICT RESOLUTION

CONNECTIONS

CREATIVITY/IMAGINATION

CULTURES

CUSTOMS

DEPENDENCE

ENTERTAINMENT

THE ENVIRONMENT

FANTASY/REALITY

FEELINGS

FRIENDSHIP

THE FUTURE

GAMES/SPORTS

GLOBAL PERSPECTIVES

GOOD AND EVIL

HERITAGE

HUMAN RIGHTS

IDENTITIES

INDEPENDENCE

INSTITUTIONS

INTEGRATION

INTERDEPENDENCE

INVENTION

INVESTIGATIONS

ISSUES

JUSTICE/FAIRNESS

LEADERSHIP

LEISURE

MODELS

NEEDS/NECESSITY

PATTERNS

PERSONAL DEVELOPMENT

PERSONAL SAFETY

PERSPECTIVES

POWER

RELATIONSHIPS

RESPONSIBILITY

RIGHTS/VALUES

RISK-TAKING/COURAGE

ROLES

RULES/LAWS

SPACE

SURVIVAL

TECHNOLOGICAL COMPETENCE

TIME

TOLERANCE

TRANSITIONS

UTOPIAS

WELL-BEING